KALEIDOSCOPE OF IDEAS

Kaleidoscope of IDEAS

HANDS-ON ACTIVITIES FOR GIFTED MINDS

HAZEL EDWARDS

© Hazel Edwards 2024

Published in 2024 by Amba Press, Melbourne, Australia.
www.ambapress.com.au

Previously published with Dr Helen McGrath, in 1999 by Horwitz Martin.

All rights reserved. No part of this book may be reproduced or transmitted in any form or by any means, electronic or mechanical, including photocopying, recording or by any information storage and retrieval system, without prior permission in writing from the publisher.

Cover design: Tess McCabe
Internal design: Amba Press
Proofreader: Sarah Fallon

ISBN: 9781923215160 (pbk)
ISBN: 9781923215177 (ebk)

A catalogue record for this book is available from the National Library of Australia.

Contents

About this book	1
The process of creative thinking	3
A kaleidoscope of ideas!	11
Aardvarks to zircons: curiosity projects	14
Abracadabra words	23
Acronymania	26
Advertising	31
Auctioneer	34
BAR	37
Bumper stickers	39
Cartoons	42
Composer	46
Create a ...	48
Curator	51
Designer	55
Devil's advocate	57
Different endings	60
Experiments and surveys	63
Frankenstein	65
Graphic stories	74
How many can you think of?	78
How many ways?	81
Jeopardy	84
Landscaping	87
Links	89

Lucky dip	91
Mergers	95
Off-beat	101
Picture this!	104
PIN numbers	107
Plotting	110
PMI (Pluses, Minuses, Intriguing aspects)	114
Postcode artist	117
POSTER! Creative problem-solving	119
Private eye	131
Recipe parodies	134
Renovator's delight	137
SAMs (Similes, Analogies, and Metaphors)	139
SCRUMPTIOUS	143
Sentencing	148
Shapemakers	152
Six Thinking Hats	155
Top five reasons	159
Tracking	163
What if …?	166
What's one of these?	168
Windows of opportunity	170
Conclusion	173
About the author	175

About this book

Few books teach creative thinking in the classroom. Since a future of constant change has been predicted for our current students, creative thinking will be a necessary tool for survival and success. The student who can problem-solve in a creative way, or create new products to meet new demands, will fare much better in this new world.

This book focuses on practical classroom activities which are user-friendly and easily implemented. Most require little preparation and can be adapted to suit other specific content at either the primary or secondary level. This is because the underlying strategies can be used systematically to develop creative thinking and are not just 'one-offs'.

Edward de Bono suggested that when teaching students to think creatively, we need to start with activities which are just 'plain fun'. Consequently, the majority of our activities offer students enjoyment and engagement. De Bono believed some activities should also be relevant to students' everyday lives (he refers to these as 'in their own backyard') or deal with larger, more global and serious issues. We start with the 'fun' activities, move to the personally relevant ones and then encourage students to tackle the more serious activities. This is the basis of ordering the activities within a topic.

Many activities require group work because students learn cooperative social skills, and co-creating allows access to the novel and effective thinking of classmates — allowing 'piggybacking' from one interesting but not-so-good idea to another better one. It is also important that students be allowed to create in an environment of psychological safety.

Cooperative group work, if correctly structured, allows for that. A 'no-putdown' rule should operate at all times. Respect for new ideas and alternative perceptions should also be conveyed at all times, and risk-taking with new ideas should be acceptable and respected behaviour.

Each of the 1,645 activities tells you:

- ❖ Aspects of creativity (see pp 3–10 for an explanation)
- ❖ Key Learning Area (KLA) focus (taken from the Curriculum and Standards Frameworks)
- ❖ Age suitability (the appropriate year levels for each topic)
- ❖ Resources and preparation (the necessary teacher preparation before beginning the topic).

A number of Templates have been included in this book. Many of them can be photocopied, written on by students and then filed away. Others can be re-used many times, as they are posters to place on the classroom table for students to use as they work. Maybe enlarge and laminate these 'Poster' Templates (denoted by a large symbol) for convenient re-use and maintenance.

Enjoy the activities and your students will respond to them with enthusiasm too.

Acknowledgement that Dr Helen Mc Grath contributed to the earlier edition of this book but is now unable to continue writing.

The process of creative thinking

Creativity is the process of making something new by imagining possibilities and/or thoughtfully linking these in novel combinations.

Creativity can be seen in:

- humour
- artwork
- performances
- solutions to a problem
- campaigns
- brochures
- arguments, theories and models
- stories
- buildings and machines
- musical creations
- systems and procedures
- fashion
- experiments and research designs.

Can we teach students to think creatively? Research evidence suggests that all students can learn to think more creatively if they are taught the skills and are given opportunities to practise those skills. Highly motivated and creative students exist who appear to need very little encouragement to discover new ways of doing things, new products and new solutions. They appear to have a 'natural' ability to think in original ways. But even they can benefit from specific training in skills which will enable them to use that ability to its fullest extent.

> *It may not be possible to train genius – but there is an awful lot of useful creativity that takes place without genius.* Edward de Bono (1993)

Following are the creative thinking skills and processes which can be built upon. Within each topic they are referred to as 'Aspect of creativity'.

1 Fluency

Fluency is about generating many different but relevant responses. Research suggests that the best and most original idea is more often found in the later ideas suggested, rather than the initial ones.

Brainstorming

Brainstorming is one example of a process based on fluency. Lots of possibilities are suggested and accepted without comment, even if some seem irrelevant at the time.

Later they are evaluated. One of the positive outcomes of brainstorming is 'hitchhiking'. This is the building upon the brainstormed ideas of others – even the discarded ones. This is co-building, not stealing others' ideas.

- List all the possible effects of allowing students to wear casual clothes instead of a uniform.
- Brainstorm all the ways a school fete could be improved.

Lists

Listing as many things as you can, which are in a specific category, is also a form of fluency, e.g. attribute listing is an example of a 'list'.

- How many songs can you list which feature a colour in the title?

Systematic Alphabetic Generation (SAG)

In this fluency technique, each letter of the alphabet is taken in combination with every other letter in order to find a solution (e.g. to try and recollect the name of something) or to increase the number of items you can list in a particular category (see Template 1, p 30).

2 Flexibility

Flexibility is about approaching things in a flexible and alternative way. It can also involve thinking of a variety of alternative ideas or interpretations.

- ◇ What else could a potato masher be used for?

3 Originality

Originality involves knowing the difference between an original idea, and an ordinary or typical idea; and producing novel or unique ideas. It can be about producing something unique which means unlike others. It can also involve combining known ideas into some new form.

- ◇ Design a new game based on the features of several games you have played.

4 Elaboration

This is the process of filling out ideas, adding interesting details or making something more complex.

- ◇ Improve a school desk to make it more appealing to a student.

5 Lateral thinking

This process involves freeing up the mind so that it does not automatically follow routine paths when seeking new ideas and solutions. If you start from a different point, rather than starting from the centre (as most people usually do), then you increase the likelihood of beginning new patterns of thinking.

- ◇ By thinking only about colours, develop a solution to the problem of young bicycle riders not wearing protective helmets.

6 Synectics

Synectics is the process of finding similarities between unrelated and seemingly disconnected ideas. In this way, new possibilities become apparent.

- How are a banana and an elephant alike?

7 Imagination

This involves projecting yourself into the feelings of others, or putting yourself in another place or time where you haven't ever been.

- Imagine a world where there is no colour, only black and white. Describe life in this world.

8 Risk-taking and curiosity

People who develop new ideas must be prepared to:

- follow their curiosity
- have the courage to expose themselves to criticism or failure
- show a willingness to express their ideas to others
- take a guess, rather than get 'hung up' on having the 'right' answer
- be prepared to defend their original ideas, solutions and products.

Students should be exposed to these attitudes and encouraged to adopt these behaviours as the basis of constructive creativity.

9 Creative problem-solving

This is a systematic process of coming up with a solution to a problem where there is no correct answer and where many solutions could work.

Details of the problem are given, and there are a number of systematic steps to be followed in pursuit of the best and most creative solution. These steps usually focus on:

- getting facts
- identifying the problems and their priorities
- generating possible solutions

- evaluating them
- choosing the best one
- working out how to implement it
- reviewing
- long-term evaluation.

10 Creative people need to think logically, too!

'Imagineers' may have good ideas, but 'innovators' put them into practice by thinking logically about the good ideas, evaluating them and then developing an action plan. Here are some of the implementation skills.

Looking at the big picture

When thinking creatively, the 'big picture' also needs to be taken into account.

- What are all the factors which must be taken into account in making a decision as to what kind of product or solution could be used?
- Who are the key people involved in the big picture and what are their perceptions and values? How will this decision/solution/idea/product affect them?

Logical thinking

The kind of logical thinking might be:

- deductive reasoning – following through the logical sequence of implications and putting pieces of logical data together
- logical application – taking an idea, model or solution and applying it accurately and logically to a specific context
- hypothetical thinking – predicting the logical implications of a given hypothetical situation identifying logical parallels and similarities between two or more things.

11 Evaluation/redirection of a new idea

Developing new ideas, solutions and products is the first step. Assessing whether they are feasible is the second step. Evaluate and/or redirect by the following strategies.

A criteria grid

The most relevant criteria are put into a grid and one or more products or solutions can be assessed/compared numerically. Criteria which may be relevant are:

- costs
- riskiness
- impact
- overall appeal
- look
- feasibility
- user friendliness
- time
- legality
- convenience
- humaneness.

Example A

To evaluate two fridge magnets, you could use this grid.

Criteria (1–5, with 5 being best)	Fridge magnet A	Fridge magnet B
Appeal (1–5)		
Durability (1–5)		
Value for money (1–5)		
Total score		

Example B

Possibilities	Criteria (1–10, with 10 being best)				Total scores
	Criteria A: Costs	Criteria B: Legality	Criteria C: Convenience	Criteria D: Humanness	
Solution 1					
Solution 2					
Solution 3					
Solution 4					

Although the criteria grid doesn't give you a direct answer as to which is best or how good something is, it does clarify thinking and assist decision-making.

Road testing

The idea, solution or product can be 'road tested'. For example:

- it can be described or shown to a number of people who give their responses to it
- the product or solution can be tried out and data can be kept.

Consequential prediction

With this process, the possible consequences of adopting a solution or idea can be identified. For example:

- What are the short-term consequences?
- What are the long-term consequences?
- What could go wrong?

- What is the best-case scenario?
- What is the worst-case scenario?
- What is the most likely outcome?

A PMI analysis or the Six Thinking Hats strategy

Either of these strategies can be used to evaluate. Both of them have been suggested by de Bono. Often when others use abbreviations the process sounds too hard. But...

PMI stands for:

Pluses

Minuses

Intriguing aspects.

The Six Thinking Hats strategy involves looking at a situation, idea, product and/or solution according to six different perspectives. These are:

- using the White Hat (the objective facts)
- using the Red Hat (emotions, feelings, hunches and intuitions)
- using the Black Hat (disadvantages, difficulties and negative realities)
- using the Yellow Hat (advantages and benefits)
- using the Green Hat (creative improvement)
- using the Blue Hat (thinking about thinking).

A kaleidoscope of ideas!

We decided to start with a 'kaleidoscope' activity to link with the title of the book. 'Kaleidoscope' may be a difficult word to spell but it's an excellent starting point for creativity. A kaleidoscope is a toy for the eyes which makes new pictures from constantly changing colours and shapes.

Creativity is a multifaceted process which can be used in many contexts. When you look through a kaleidoscope, much depends upon the perspective or angle from which the colours and shapes are seen, and how long you look. Similarly, when the human brain or imagination plays around with new combinations of old or new idea-shapes to solve problems creatively, the shaping process is similar. However, those novel combinations need to be evaluated to see if they work.

Creative tasks

In pairs, students can research or try any or several of the following tasks.

ASPECT OF CREATIVITY
- Curiosity
- Flexibility
- Imagination
- Logical thinking (deductive reasoning, hypothetical thinking)

KLA FOCUS
- English
- SOSE
- Mathematics
- Science
- Health and Physical Education
- Arts
- Music

AGE SUITABILITY
- Years 3–9

RESOURCES AND PREPARATION
- A kaleidoscope to play with!

- Kaleidoscopic means showing constant change. What is the derivation of the word kaleidoscope? Which language claims it? In what way was it first used? Who designed the first kaleidoscope? Make up some new words with the 'kaleid-' beginning.

- Who or what is the Mandelbrott Set? (Clue: fractals)

- 'I dream in fractals, constantly changing colours in recurring shapes, like the repetitive shapes in nature.' (Dreamer). Survey the class to find out how many students dream in colour/in black and white/in abstract/not in pictures.

- 'Chroma' means 'the quality of colour'. In pairs, students can list as many words which come from this meaning as they can find, e.g. chromatic, chromatography. Have them make up some of their own 'chroma' words.

- Within our world, there are people who can only perceive in black and white. Is it possible to have a concept of a colour, without seeing it, e.g. you understand the meaning of 'red' but haven't experienced 'redness'? How would you explain 'green' to a person who does not see colour? How would football clubs design their tops and shorts if all the supporters only saw in black and white?

- What causes a person to be colour-blind? Why are red and green difficult for those who are colour-blind? Is there any connection between colour-blindness, gender and genetics? Use colour-blindness as a plot device in a short play.

- If we all see the same shades, how is it possible for people to have 'favourite colours'? What makes us comfortable with certain colours and depressed by others? Why, and in what ways do supermarkets use yellow and green to attract shoppers?

- There are many stories of good fortune linked with rainbows, e.g. a pot of gold at the end of the rainbow, seeing a rainbow is good luck. What other 'good luck' stories can you find out about? Rainbows tend to appear after short showers. Why?

- Make your own kaleidoscopes.

- Organise a class display.
- Create a story where there is a kaleidoscope clue.
- Organise a kaleidoscopic fashion parade called 'The Big K'.
- Take a good look at a kaleidoscope. Then draw its pieces and how it works.

VARIATIONS AND FOLLOW-UP

- Students can design a kaleidoscopic scarf for someone who loves multi colours and another for a person who is colour-blind. Will the patterns be different? Why?
- Students can draw a fractal and explain its composition. In what ways are fractals used in industry?

Aardvarks to zircons: curiosity projects

Most projects set for students are predictable and sometimes boring — requiring little to no creativity. A 'good' project taps into students' curiosity; stimulates excitement about learning; and provides students with a strong motivation to research, find answers and create new things. Teachers don't have to know all the answers before setting this type of project. Their role is to focus on good strategies for finding out, and to help students generate well thought out alternative answers.

Such a project has the following 'ideal' features:

- ◆ an unusual topic which still relates back to the main area of study
- ◆ use of unusual research skills beyond using just the library and the Internet
- ◆ specific questions which range from basic factual knowledge to open-ended interpretation and speculation (using Bloom's model of levels of thinking)

ASPECT OF CREATIVITY
- Curiosity
- Creative problem-solving (some of these answers require more than library or Internet research)
- Flexibility
- Imagination
- Logical thinking (deductive reasoning, hypothetical thinking)

KLA FOCUS
- English
- SOSE
- Mathematics
- Science
- Health and Physical Education
- Arts
- Music

AGE SUITABILITY
- Years 3–9

RESOURCES AND PREPARATION
- Provide training in research and interviewing skills.

- intriguing sounding words and phrases
- a focus on unusual angles and the more bizarre elements
- some personal relevance
- a fascinating title, e.g. 'The Mystery of History' or one which sounds impressive, e.g. 'Forensic Science'
- a variety of ways in which the information and ideas can be presented, e.g. on location, in costume, using multi-media, involving the audience, using a guest speaker, giving a demonstration, distributing samples.

Curiosity projects to explore

Highways and byways

- How are streets named? What are the rules?
- How might they be named? Is there a better system?
- What are the rules for the location of post-boxes and phones in streets?
- What funny names for houses have you observed?
- Research numbering systems and anomalies.
- Find weird collections of names for street groups or estates.
- What are the differences between streets, lanes, roads, avenues, freeways, highways, clearways, dead-ends, expressways, laneways, crescents, courts, walks, lanes, squares, etc.? Specify the rules and make a poster.
- Photograph (for a display) funny letterboxes, street names and house names.

Going places: international conundrums

- If you were born in an aeroplane, what would your nationality be — that of your parents'/the country you were flying over/the country to which the plane belonged/where your birth was registered?
- If you were born under water in a submarine, what would your nationality be?

- How does the International Date Line operate?
- What if you have a birthday while crossing the International Date Line – would you have two birthdays or none (depending upon which direction you are travelling)?
- Passport rules – what are they? Design a better Australian passport and passport system.
- What attempts have been made to establish a common currency (e.g. Eurodollar) and language (e.g. Esperanto)? Is it a good idea?

Lingua animalia: animal communication
- Do birds and animals have a language?
- How do different types of animals communicate with each other?
- If we could teach animals to speak, what would they learn?
- Design a dictionary for an animal.
- What does research say about whether apes and gorillas can be taught human language?
- Write a story about a pet who is able to speak to its owner.

Pyrotechnics
- How do fireworks work?
- What is a pyrotechnician's job?
- How are computers used with pyrotechnics?
- Apart from celebrations, where else might fireworks be used?
- What are the natural 'fireworks' of life?
- Why is it so difficult to take photos of fireworks?
- Select music and design a sound and light show.

What a job! Professional testers
- What kind of people test these things? What skills would they need? How might they test the following?
    - chocolate
    - wine/beer/cider
    - parachutes

- guide dogs
- breath
- safety equipment.

◊ What's the difference between a taster and a tester?

◊ Create a script featuring two testers with one claiming to be allergic to the product being tested.

A vegetable aficionado!

◊ List all the fruit and vegetable phrases that you can think of, e.g. As cool as a cucumber'.

◊ Research grafting, genetic engineering with fruit and vegetables, and chemical spraying versus organic growing procedures.

◊ Why do some people hate brussels sprouts? (Do a survey first, to identify the vegetables people dislike most.)

◊ Create vegetables with different colours or shapes.

◊ Make animals from vegetables, fruits and natural products such as rice, wheat, leaves, etc.

◊ Do a PMI (see p 114) on 'mini-vegetables'.

◊ How could we encourage more students to eat vegetables? List as many strategies as you can think of.

◊ Create a game based on vegetables.

Customer loyalty schemes

◊ What is one 'frequent flyer' point worth in terms of money? (Choose any scheme to investigate.) What procedure did you use and why?

◊ Outline the best way to use a 'frequent flyer' scheme from the customer's perspective.

◊ With what other industries could customer loyalty schemes operate?

◊ How could you use a customer loyalty scheme in your school?

Pets and more pets

- How do pet cemeteries work?
- What do pet psychologists do?
- What happens at pet 'holiday camps'?
- Investigate the roles of pet-sitters and pet-walkers.
- Create new travel harnesses and leashes, and travel boxes for pets.
- Create new names for pet food, e.g. 'Bow Wow Chow'.
- Design a sales campaign for a virtual pet, e.g. a pet rock.
- What kind of psychological problems could a domestic pet have? Build a story around one.
- How would your life change if you were given an aardvark as a pet?

Graveyards

- How many people get buried compared to cremated?
- Can you be buried on your own property or only in special locations?
- Are compulsory pre-paid funerals a good idea?
- How is a cemetery map organised so people can find the right graves? (By religion/alphabetical order/age/headstones/streets?)
- Create the perfect cemetery.
- Analyse the topic of compulsory pre-paid funerals.

Wills and won'ts

- How do wills operate? Can a will be written on something other than paper?
- What happens if someone doesn't have a will when they die?
- Who usually inherits?
- What is a 'codicil'?
- What is 'primogeniture'?
- What does an executor do?
- How old do you have to be before you can write a will?
- Can you set terms and conditions in your will such as, 'if my wife remarries, she can't inherit' or 'if anyone disputes my will they can't inherit'?

- What are the rules for witnessing the signing of a will?
- Create a script or a story about a funny will.
- If a distant relative left you a zircon mine overseas, what impact would that have on your life?

Circuses
- Are there any restrictions on animals performing?
- How long does it take to set up the circus tents, etc.
- How are performers trained, e.g. clowns, trapeze artists?
- Do circuses carry insurance? What sort?
- What are the major types of animals used in circuses?
- What's the difference between a circus and a stage show?
- How did the 'Big Top' get its name?
- Is there a regular route for a circus? How do they travel over water?
- How could the lions get their exercise? List as many ways as you can think of.
- What other kinds of circuses can you think of?
- Write a mystery story set in a circus in which an animal is part of the plot.

Bionic body parts
- Which parts of the human body can now be replaced bionically?
- Should animals be entitled to bionic replacements? Which ones? Why?
- How should these parts be costed?
- Create an animal cartoon character who has bionic parts but who isn't really 'super'.

Chocolate
- Who made the first chocolate?
- What is the most expensive chocolate in the world?
- What is chocolate made from?
- How many chocaholic societies exist?

- Are there chocaholic tours in your neighbourhood? Where might they go? Draw a map.
- A chocolate newspaper with milk-choc ink was made for chocaholics to read and eat. Suggest news items to be included in the paper.

Car names
- How are car names chosen?
- What do some car names suggest?
- List other ways car names could be chosen.
- Design and draw a new car, motorbike or item of transport. Give it a new name and an advertising campaign.

Mazes and labyrinths
- Is maze design an occupation? Does it have a title?
- What is the function of a maze? What are the key design principles?
- Are there any safety features in mazes?
- What are the most common materials/dimensions used?
- Design a maze as your playground.
- Design a maze for your pet.

X-rays
- Why are they called 'X' rays?
- Are they rays?
- For what purposes are X-rays taken?
- Are there any dangers attached to having or being exposed to many X-rays?
- How are X-rays used at airports and with food?
- Create a story about an X-ray mix-up.

Magic
- Is there always a logical explanation for 'magic'?
- What are some of the rules of magic?

- Research wizards, witches, shamans, illusionists. If the witches were the women of 'wit', what did they know?
- Prepare a magic show. See if others can explain your tricks.
- Learn two card tricks and perform them. Make one up.
- List ways in which a magician could be usefully employed in a school.
- Find as many 'magic' phrases as you can and explain where they came from, e.g. 'abracadabra', 'shazam', 'open sesame', etc.

Tents

- Why does a tent stay up? What are the basic scientific principles involved?
- Research 'tent cities'.
- What are major differences between a wigwam, yurt, gazebo, marquee and mia mia?
- What kinds of tents are used in high altitudes and why?
- Create a perfect tent for yourself and a friend.

Animation

- How are cartoons animated?
- If drawn manually, how long would one minute of animation take to draw?
- How is the illusion of movement created?
- Who owns characters such as Mickey Mouse?
- What is meant by copyright? What is a patent? What is intellectual property?
- Make a 'flip cartoon' book (see p 42).
- Compare two animated TV shows and evaluate them in terms of what you consider to be the most important criteria, e.g. colour, drawing, mouth movement, etc.

Lost and found

- Who owns lost property?
- What skills are needed by search-and-rescue squads?

- Who pays the costs after a search-and-rescue attempt?
- Are there any differences between missing and lost?
- How many 'missing persons' get found?
- Create a perfect lost-and-found system for your school.
- Design a user-friendly and efficient lost-property box.

Hoaxes

- Research famous hoaxes, e.g. a Sydney radio station spent considerable on-air time discussing the 'jumbo' which was to fit under the Sydney Harbour Bridge that day. At one minute before noon, a ferry with an inflated plastic pink elephant sailed under the bridge!
- What's the difference between a joke and a hoax?
- Share a hoax or practical joke. Interview parents, grandparents or elderly neighbours about any hoaxes or practical jokes which they can remember.
- What positive and negative impact can a hoax or practical joke have on other people?
- Research the beginnings of April Fools' Day on 1 April.
- Why is it accepted that after midday, the joke is turned back on the joker who is then considered the April fool'?
- Research court jesters. Design or make a jester's costume.
- What or who are the equivalents of court jesters in today's society?

VARIATIONS AND FOLLOW-UP

- To gather ideas for other topics, use an A-to-Z approach, i.e. list all the letters of the alphabet on a sheet of paper and ask students (in groups of three or four) to generate ideas under each letter.
- Establish a 'curiosity bank', i.e. a box in which students can deposit interesting topics or questions around which to research or develop a project.

Abracadabra words

Our version of 'lateral thinking' is 'abracadabra words'. They help students to think laterally about a problem or task by forcing them to think outside the normal boundaries. It's a 'random word strategy' where a word is selected at random and all associations with it are used to think of new ideas to solve a problem.

Edward de Bono proposed the concept of lateral thinking: where the mind is forced to go down a different and unpredictable path in order to create new connections and new directions. People rarely come up with new ideas if they stay on their usual 'mental paths'.

Students use a word selected at random to think laterally about a problem or task. They should undertake the task initially with no prompts. Then, when they have reached the point where they can't think of any new or better ideas, they try again — this time using the random word.

Students are given the task of finding ways to improve the school fete.

ASPECT OF CREATIVITY
- Lateral thinking
- Fluency (listing, brainstorming)

KLA FOCUS
- English
- Science
- SOSE

AGE SUITABILITY
- Years 3–9

RESOURCES AND PREPARATION
- A dictionary.
- Model the process.

After brainstorming the possibilities, they are then given the random word 'comfort' to use, and, making word associations from it, they address the same problem. This process can be repeated with a number of random words.

Ways to find a random word

- One student identifies any page number of a dictionary, e.g. page 17. Another student selects a number between 1 and 30, e.g. 3. Therefore, the third word on the seventeenth page of the dictionary becomes the random word to be used. Books other than a dictionary can be used, but you would then need to select a page, a line and a number from 1 to about 13 in order to select the word in the line. The random word should be a noun. If the selected word is not a noun, select the next noun after it.
- A fun but time consuming way is to ask each student to write down any four nouns. Remove duplications and come up with a sheet of sixty words which are numbered from 1 to 60. At the point where you are ready to select the word, note the reading of the second hand on a student's watch, e.g. it might be 31 seconds – now select the 31st word on the list. Develop several such lists, and alternate and replace them over time.
- Blindfold a student and have them 'finger jab' at a randomly opened page of a book. If the word located is not a noun, select the next noun in the line. Quickest way.

Task ideas

- As health and safety officer you're worried about shop food going bad in refrigerators and on shelves when not sold by the expiry date. Devise a way of checking these dates so it is easier for the shopkeepers to control. Use diagrams.
- How can water consumption be reduced?
- How can a local council get people to use the litter bins instead of dropping rubbish in the strip shopping centre, and at parks and picnic grounds?

- How can we move cars more quickly on the road in peak hours?
- How can we get children to eat more vegetables?
- How many ways could we entertain five-year-old children at a party for less than ten dollars?
- How could we match people who want part-time work with vacancies that are available?
- How can we reward people who are the originators of good ideas? Think of as many ways as you can.
- How many uses can you think of for empty containers?

VARIATIONS AND FOLLOW-UP

- This strategy can also be used with 'How many can you think of?' (see p 78) and 'How many ways?' (see p 81).
- Ask students to think of alternative ways to select 'abracadabra words'.

Acronymania

Acronymania is a real word! It means 'having a passion for forming acronyms' or 'the craze of forming acronyms'.

People talk of the efficiency of the KISS principle. KISS stands for Keep It Simple, Stupid. RICE is an acronym for immediate treatment of a sports injury (Rest Ice Compression Elevation). We rather like the SKIN movement, i.e. Spend Kids Inheritances Now!

You can take some liberties with acronyms, but the word that is used should recall the words or sentences within it. An acronym can be both a memory and a teaching device. Each letter can stand for an associated idea to direct thinking. Alternatively, each letter can stand for a word which assists memorisation of concepts or steps in a skill.

Creating an acronym requires high-level creative thinking and problem-solving skills, plus logical thinking. Fitting ideas into a combination of letters which make

ASPECT OF CREATIVITY
- Fluency (Systematic Alphabetic Generation)
- Logical thinking (logical application)
- Evaluation (road testing)

KLA FOCUS
- English
- Science
- Arts
- Mathematics
- Music
- SOSE
- LOTE
- Health and Physical Education

AGE SUITABILITY
- Years 3–9

RESOURCES AND PREPARATION
- Show examples of good acronyms.
- Discuss how and why they work.
- Stress that some acronyms direct or describe behaviour while others help you remember important facts or steps.

a complete word is a challenging task. This activity also develops an understanding of synonyms, and encourages the use of a dictionary and thesaurus.

Stress that some acronyms direct or describe behaviour while others help you remember important facts or steps.

An acronym is more than an acrostic poem. In an acrostic poem you just think of descriptive words starting with each letter that connect to the topic and write them in. Here is an example of an acrostic poem:

Soft

Numbing

Overwhelming

Wintry.

There are no core concepts or steps, just descriptive words.

Here is another example of an acronym.

Action words work, or nouns with impact

Collect key words and phrases and brainstorm alternatives

Refer to a dictionary or thesaurus

Organise systematic alphabetical combinations to get ideas for new words

Note each skill and choose one word for each

'**Y**es' or 'No' on each word – select the best one

Match key words and phrases to each letter

The acronym CAMPING can teach some of the rules of camping in a form that students can easily remember. If it is rehearsed, it can also help them to remember what to do in the setting.

Clear area near tent and dig a trench

Access to water needed

Make a fire from dry, light wood

Protect food from insects and sun

Inspect site for dangerous features

Nature needs respecting. Take nothing but photos, leave only footprints

Ground hole for bush toilet

Possible acronyms

Ideas for suitable acronyms are listed below. However, students may wish to select their own.

- Encourage road safety on a poster (WATCH, BEWARE, STAY SAFE)
- Remind about electrical safety (SHOCK)
- Encourage healthy eating (EAT WELL)
- Encourage exercise (KEEP FIT)
- Remember first-aid procedures (FIRST AID, ASSIST)
- Teach about boating safety (WATERCARE)
- Remind people about pet care (PET CARE)
- Instruct people on how to make origami (ORIGAMI)
- Show how to care for bonsai (small Japanese plants) (MINI PLANT).

VARIATIONS AND FOLLOW-UP

- Students can create and practise acronyms to remember key information in a current topic.
- This is a good way to learn for examinations. Students can develop acronyms to remember core concepts – each letter standing for one aspect.
- Students can also use acronym sentences where they list the key concepts or elements, and then make up a sentence starting with those letters, e.g. to remember that the four main characters in a

novel were Jane, Amanda, Sandra and Sam, students could use the acronymic sentence:

Just

Ask

Someone

Stupid

The more bizarre or personally relevant the sentence, the more likely it is to be remembered.

⋄ Template 1 (see p 30) outlines the steps used in making an acronym. This will give students a formula to follow when they create acronyms.

TEMPLATE 1
TO CREATE AN ACRONYM

A Arrange the steps or directions in order. Select the key words and phrases in each step or instruction.

C Check the dictionary or thesaurus to find replacement words which mean the same thing (synonyms), e.g. for the word 'draw' you could write 'sketch' or 'picture'.

R Rearrange the starting letters of each key word or phrase. Do they look like any word you know that has something to do with what you are trying to teach? (e.g. if you are teaching how to make a mobile, do the letters look like they make the word MOBILE or HANGING?) Find a word and put statements against the letters you can easily fill. Now brainstorm all the words that you can think of to go with each unfilled letter. Are any suitable?

O Organise a SAG search (Systematic Alphabetical Generation) to find words and phrases to fill the leftover letters. One way to generate possible words is to add each of the five vowels to each starting consonant, e.g. if one unfilled letter was 'P' you could try 'Pa' words, then 'Pe' words, then 'Pi' words, etc. Or, you could go the other way and generate words by trying each starting vowel with all the consonants in alphabetical order, e.g. if a leftover vowel was 'A', you could try 'Ab' words, then 'Ac' words, etc.

N Nouns and verbs work best (especially verbs) as the first word in a phrase because they are more easily remembered, e.g. choose, refer, dig, collect, number, etc. General verbs such as 'get', or 'put' do not work quite as well, as they are easily forgotten.

Y Your acronym should make sense and cover all the important steps. Go through it and check.

M Make sure it works for other people, too. When you are happy with your acronym, give it to another group without explaining, and ask them later if it made sense and helped them to do what you were trying to teach.

Please note: Sometimes you can start with a good word and then fit the steps around it. Then you can leave out the 'R' step.

Advertising

Ask students to create an advertising campaign that introduces them to many different areas such as TV, publicity, jingles, voice-overs, graphics, merchandising, endorsements, print media, radio, billposters, etc. This allows students to be creative in the way these areas are tackled, as they need to create ideas and images which are both effective and novel.

Advertising campaigns

Students create advertising campaigns for specific purposes. They can focus on:

- budget, e.g. give them a budget for advertising the school dance
- market research required
- audience sampling, e.g. testing it out on typical people
- target audience/buyers
- products and merchandising, e.g. badges, brochures, fridge magnets, billboards, bumper stickers, etc.

ASPECT OF CREATIVITY
- Originality
- Flexibility
- Looking at the big picture (consider all the people, consider all the factors)
- Evaluation (road testing)

KLA FOCUS
- English
- Arts
- Technology
- Health and Physical Education
- SOSE
- Science
- Mathematics
- Music

AGE SUITABILITY
- Years 3–9

RESOURCES AND PREPARATION
- Discuss and demonstrate effective advertising campaigns from newspapers, billboards, pamphlets, fridge magnets, merchandising, TV, radio, etc.
- In groups, ask students to analyse and evaluate the above, and then draw out guiding principles.
- Discuss the concept of market research.
- Investigate the concept of 'controversial' advertising.

- actors for TV and radio ads and voice-overs
- graphics
- logos
- ethical issues (identify and address)
- rental space and locations
- jingles, TV and radio ads.

Students 'road test' their campaign or product on different age groups, and write a report on the impact of their campaign or product.

Advertising ideas

Here are some ideas to advertise:

- a biofeedback watch which lets you know the intensity of any emotion you are experiencing
- an electric potato/carrot/apple peeler
- airtime (for your own show or for an ad) on a school radio station
- advertising space on school backpacks
- time-sharing, e.g. a pet, a car, a parent, a child, a brother or sister
- a small, portable device for estimating pollen levels
- automatic pet feeders for when you are not there
- a device for testing the purity of drinking water
- sun protection for albinos or those with no skin pigment
- selling the political idea of a dictatorship to free minded people
- mobility aids for people who are blind
- 'tourist air' (in spray cans) from unusual locations
- a recycled present shop
- a vaccination against boredom
- less sleep per night
- an umbrella which converts to a shopping bag
- face washers or doorknobs.

VARIATIONS AND FOLLOW-UP

- Link what is being advertised with a current topic, or with school events such as sports day, fete, school dance, school radio station, etc.

- Students can research/debate these issues:
    - sportspeople endorsing products
    - subliminal advertising
    - indirect advertising through product placement in movies
    - advertising on the back of toilet doors and on toilet rolls
    - students being allowed to accept advertising on school bags
    - using rewards offered by companies such as McDonalds to encourage children to read more at school or to enter writing competitions.

Auctioneer

Auctions have a high curiosity value for many students. There is something exciting and dangerous about the speed and choices. This activity asks students to research how auctions operate and then to role-play various kinds of auctions which are relevant to their real world. The creative aspect is in adapting the idea to different circumstances and in the dramatic performance of an auction. There is also a great deal of artistic creativity in the promotion of the auction, and the production of the catalogue and currency.

Explain the concept of an auction as buying and selling through public bidding. Buyers are allowed to look at the goods beforehand. The auctioneer's role is to enthuse the audience and sell to the highest bidder. The audience keeps offering higher bids, until the highest bid is accepted.

Mock auction

◊ One student becomes an auctioneer who will sell the items to the highest

ASPECT OF CREATIVITY
- Curiosity
- Originality
- Flexibility
- Logical thinking (logical application)

KLA FOCUS
- Mathematics
- English
- SOSE
- Arts
- Technology

AGE SUITABILITY
- Years 3–9

RESOURCES AND PREPARATION
- A hammer.
- Mock money for bids.

bidder. Point out that an auctioneer's job is to make the items sound attractive or relevant. Before the auction takes place students will need to:
- design a catalogue
- number and name each item or 'lot'.

❖ Students can design and make their own currency and as a class, give it a name. Students will need to decide:
- How much of the currency will each student receive?
- Does the basic amount received have to be earned?
- Can extra be earned? If so, how? (e.g. extra work, improved test performance, early submission of work)
- How will the currency be stored?
- Will there be a banker?
- How will the banking system work?
- What will the bank be called?
- Will credit be used?

❖ Hold the mock auction in the classroom accepting bids for a range of goods and services such as:
- artwork done by students
- poems
- hours of work/play, e.g. one hour of playing a popular game.
- classroom jobs
- additional support, e.g. half an hour's assistance on a computer game
- second-hand items from home that have no real monetary value but may appeal to students.

VARIATIONS AND FOLLOW-UP

❖ Students can attend an auction to see how one works, e.g. house, livestock, art, car, customs, railway lost property, police auctions, etc. Research projects and reports can follow the excursion.

❖ Students can research and put together a 'Dutch auction'.

- As a follow-up, students can engage in creative project management, e.g. they can come up with ideas for a novel fund-raising auction and then organise it. Fund-raising ideas could be to organise and collect old painted and autographed sneakers belonging to sports stars, jeans painted by famous artists, and books autographed by authors and/or illustrators.
- Video/record the auction performance.
- A large department store chain used their own in-house currency to encourage staff to use the sentence, 'How may I help you?' Each time a manager observed a salesperson using that phrase, they received a store dollar. Then, every month, staff could use their currency to bid at an in-house auction for goods from the store which had been returned in less than pristine condition, were left over after a sale, had been slightly damaged, were discontinued, etc. Students can discuss this concept in terms of its potential effectiveness and then apply it to their own school situation. Discuss what the teachers could 'set up' to encourage certain behaviours in students.
- Give each group of four students a set amount of money and then have the auctioneer sell the following 'outcomes' in life. Each group should have a chance to discuss their choices first, before they bid. All groups have to make at least two purchases from the list below:
  - fame
  - wealth
  - a happy and long-lasting marriage
  - well-adjusted and happy children
  - being the person who makes a great discovery which alters the future of humanity in a positive way
  - winning an Olympic medal
  - writing a best-selling novel
  - never being sick
  - travelling all over the world
  - obtaining high-level qualifications
  - owning their own business
  - having a lot of good and loyal friends.

BAR

BAR is a simple acronym which helps students to structure their thinking on how to improve something, e.g. a product or piece of equipment. In the trialling we have done, students found it easier to think creatively with the prompt of an acronym such as this.

The aim is to improve an item or make it more saleable by using the following acronym:

B Make some aspect bigger or smaller

A Add or subtract one aspect

R Rearrange one aspect

Item – a scarecrow:

B Make it three metres tall so that it sticks out above a tall crop.

A Add a wing-flap-activated voice-tape which says 'Buzz off!'

R Put scary faces on its feet as well as on its head.

ASPECT OF CREATIVITY
- Elaboration

KLA FOCUS
- Technology

AGE SUITABILITY
- Years 3–9

RESOURCES AND PREPARATION
- Model the process before you start, using the example of a school chair.

Possible things to BAR

- sink
- refrigerator
- newspaper
- suitcase
- running shoes
- key ring
- slipper
- spaghetti or salad bowl
- can-opener
- diary
- child's toy (select one from home)
- bike helmet
- backpack
- watch
- birdcage
- fishbowl
- garden gnome
- cosmetic bag
- car
- favourite toy
- umbrella

VARIATIONS AND FOLLOW-UP

- Choose an item which fits in with a current topic, e.g. the Olympics – students could be asked to BAR the Australian team's uniform or the Olympic Village.
- Students can select their own item to BAR.

Bumper stickers

Bumper stickers appeal to all of us, especially if they are witty.

We particularly like those which 'speak to' certain people about their experiences. For example:

> *Take your revenge. Live long enough to be an embarrassment to your children.*

> *If I am a stay-at-home mum, how come I spend so much time in the car?*

> *Insanity is inherited.*
> *You get it from your children.*

There is creative humour in bumper stickers and the trick is to make a point in a witty not bitter or attacking way.

ASPECT OF CREATIVITY
- Logical thinking (logical application, analogical thinking)
- Originality

KLA FOCUS
- English
- Technology
- Arts

AGE SUITABILITY
- Years 4–9

RESOURCES AND PREPARATION
- For a week, students collect examples of bumper stickers and display them on the main door of the classroom or on the ceiling.
- Students analyse what makes a good bumper sticker.

Bumper stickers for occupations and personal concerns

❖ Students can make up their own witty bumper stickers about jobs. Stress that vulgar or crude stickers are not acceptable. They must use a witty play-on-words, e.g. Old teachers never die, they just lose their class.' Using the same sentence stem as above, 'Old _____ never die, they just _____', have the students use the following occupations to make their own bumper stickers.

- Plumber
- sandwich maker
- courier
- sports coach
- train driver
- carpet cleaner
- gardener
- computer programmer
- vet
- mortician
- health and safety inspector
- fashion designer
- photographer
- pet walker
- manicurist for a bul's toenails
- a job done by one of your family
- doctor
- nurse
- the job you would like/hope to have
- specialty cake-decorator

❖ Ask students to write down some of their shared personal concerns. Then, with a partner, have them create a humorous bumper sticker around one.
The following are some common concerns many students have:
- a little brother/sister who is a pest
- lack of money

- overly strict parents
- the pain of homework.

They could use one of the following sentence stems when constructing their bumper sticker.

'If ____ then how come ____.'

'Unlike ____ I ____.'

'I may be ____ but ____.'

VARIATIONS AND FOLLOW-UP

- Organise a ceremony where students present their bumper sticker to someone who is in that job. They can design the invitations.
- Students can create appropriate shapes for bumper stickers, or design (and perhaps make) a key ring, fridge magnet, bookmark, etc.
- Students can research and collect good examples of clever graffiti. They can photograph these examples.
- Students can debate the notion that all toilet doors should have blackboards on the back.
- Researchers have developed a tactic for analysing graffiti signatures on walls so that the originators can be identified and prosecuted. Debate whether this is likely to be effective in reducing graffiti.
- Students can debate whether spray painting 'artists' are vandals or true artists.
- Students can categorise collected/observed graffiti into various kinds, e.g. political, racist.
- Place a display board in an appropriate place, e.g. the corridor and encourage students to continue to collect good examples of both bumper stickers and graffiti.

Cartoons

Students love cartoons! Few can resist their appeal. They can draw their own cartoons, make a flip cartoon book, write and draw caption cartoons or fill in blank cartoons with dialogue. The creative aspect is in either the drawings or the humorous sequences and punch lines.

Cartoon-making

There are several ways cartoons can be produced.

- Students draw their own cartoon around a theme, using a single frame, two frames, three frames or four frames.

- Students make a flip cartoon book from soft cardboard to produce a crude 'moving picture'. There are several steps they will need to follow:
  - Students will need to draw ten frames, each about the size of a business card.
  - The first frame must be very different to the tenth.

ASPECT OF CREATIVITY
- Originality
- Imagination
- Evaluation (road testing)

KLA FOCUS
- Technology
- Arts
- English

AGE SUITABILITY
- Years 2–12

RESOURCES AND PREPARATION
- Collect sample cartoons, both single- and multiple-frame for analysis.

- There must be an obvious action and change across the ten frames.
- Each successive frame must contain the same picture with very small changes in the direction of the tenth frame.
- A story board should be used to design the changes in each frame.
- Use a photocopy of the previous frame as a guide.
- The expressions on the faces of the characters (one or two at the most) must also slowly change with each frame.
- Staple the flip book at the shorter end with two staples.
- Topic suggestions are:
    - 'Food Bites' (where food has revenge)
    - 'Sports Moves' (about an athlete in training where something goes wrong).

❖ Students select a cartoon strip and white-out the dialogue. They can then photocopy it and re-do the dialogue with a new story angle.

❖ Students draw a picture to go with a selected one-frame caption such as:
- 'On the Internet, nobody knows you're a mouse.'
- 'The grass is never greener on the other side.'

❖ Students are given a single-frame cartoon and are asked to give it a humorous caption.

The acronym on Template 2 (see p 45) will help direct students in creating cartoon strips.

VARIATIONS AND FOLLOW-UP

- Have a 'cartoon corridor' exhibition or a 'cartoon of the week' corner.
- Exhibit cartoons around a theme which relates to a school event, e.g. sports day, exams, school fete, etc.
- A group can develop a cartoon character which relates to the name of the school, e.g. Al the Alvinwood Kid' (for Alvinwood Primary School).
- Students can use computer graphic programs to create cartoon characters.

TEMPLATE 2
CREATING CARTOONS

C   Consider your punch line first

A   Animals or Insects make good characters

R   Repeat your drawings in each frame and make small changes each time

T   Trial it, get feedback and redraw/rewrite

O   Open eyes to show expression

O   One character should be dominant

N   No unnecessary bits

S   Simple drawings and dialogue work best

Composer

By giving students specific 'briefs' for creatively composing music, we make the creating of sound less threatening, especially to those students who have not had musical training.

Composing ideas

In the following activities students are asked to compose original music, songs, raps, sound effects or jingles.

They can work individually, with a partner, or in groups of three or four.

⋄ Classical composer Elgar created the 'Enigma Variations' where each piece was based on the personality of one of his friends. They were identified only by initials which were attached to each piece. Students can compose a piece of music to fit the personality of a friend or a member of their family. How would they convey an explosive, short-tempered personality; or, a calm, reflective, thoughtful personality with a quirky sense of humour?

ASPECT OF CREATIVITY
- Originality

KLA FOCUS
- Music
- English
- Technology

AGE SUITABILITY
- Years 3–9

RESOURCES AND PREPARATION
- Various homemade and commercial instruments.
- Digital recorders.

- Students compose a 'Jungle Jingle' or a 'Zingle' (a zoo jingle) to sell the attractions of human tourists to jungle animals. They can choose a specific animal's viewpoint.
- Students compose a 'rap' which is a door alarm – it raps to alert the occupant to visitors. When someone rings the doorbell, the rap plays.
- Students create and perform personalised answering machine messages for people with unusual occupations. Consideration needs to be given to the length of the message, background music, voices, etc.
- From SFX (special effects) such as a door bang, wheel scream, whistle, etc. students create and perform a sound scenario for a suspenseful mystery (without a grisly murder), and provide the solution at the end, in sound.
- Students can create and perform:
  - a dialogue in music between an adolescent and a parent
  - a dawn chorus featuring the sounds likely to be heard early in the morning.
- Students tape-record machinery sounds and put together a 'guess the machine' tape. This could also be done with beach, animal, domestic, railway and fast-food sounds. Many sounds from various locations could be taped to produce a 'SFX Quiz'.
- Students create and perform:
  - a factory rap
  - an argument in music
  - a jingle to advertise 'thinking' as the new fashion in exercise
  - birthday lyrics for a special friend
  - a series of funny announcements at a transport depot, e.g. an airport, a bus depot, a train station.
- Students can work in groups to make up and perform an equivalent to Peter and the Wolf, e.g. 'Adam and the Elephant', 'Emma and the Penguin'.

VARIATIONS AND FOLLOW-UP

- Students can incorporate computer sound effects into their composition.

Create a ...

This strategy requires students to create an original machine, product, object, system or venue which meets a specific purpose.

Project ideas

Remind students to consider all the factors when they are creating their new product or system. Students can undertake one or more of the following projects.

- Work out a new (non-metric) system for measuring a person's height. What will be the new unit of measurement? A finger? An icy pole stick? Something else?
- Redesign time on a decimal scale. Make time go decimal, i.e. ten hours in a day.
- Use diagrams to explain how this will work in real-life situations like school, business and home. Benefits? Challenges?
- Plan a currency for a new country. What denominations of notes and coins

ASPECT OF CREATIVITY
- Flexibility
- Originality
- Risk-taking
- Evaluation
- Looking at the big picture (consider all factors)

KLA FOCUS
- Mathematics
- Arts
- Technology

AGE SUITABILITY
- Years 3–9

RESOURCES AND PREPARATION
- No special resources or preparation required.

will there be? Is bartering an option? Or will you use some other system? What will denominations of the currency be called? What will the currency be made from? Who will control distribution? How much of the currency will you need?

- Create an 'Opal Bank'. Suddenly, the opal is the most valuable commodity in the world. But under extreme heat or cold it can split and lessen in value. You have been commissioned to set up the 'Intergalactic Opal Bank'. If opal is to replace gold as the basis of world exchange, what problems might arise in the Antarctic or on the Equator? How could you prevent the opal being used in extreme heat or cold? Write a report which contains your recommendations.
- Compose and perform a piece of music using a new type of notation. Invite someone else to perform it from your notes.
- You've won the contract to design a maze for the 'World Garden Exhibition' in the year 2060. On average, it should take people at least ten minutes to get out of the maze. Design the basic shape. What materials will you use for the walls/barriers/hedges of the maze? Estimate the amounts of materials needed for the entire maze. What surprises could you build in? How about secret gates for rescuing distressed people? Include at least four dead-ends. Make a model of your maze.
- Create one of these special purpose machines or venues:
  - a machine which pays your bills
  - a more interactive but safe zoo
  - a spectacular birthday party venue
  - a museum for sacred tribal objects which mustn't be seen
  - a 'friendly' machine
  - a gallery for bad paintings.
- Invent a device to be used in a basketball clinic to teach basic skills such as dribbling, passing and shooting.
- Build or design a 'homework guru' or 'robo-sage' that provides answers to difficult questions.
- Build a dog kennel not using conventional materials.

- Design a mini-golf course with unusual obstacles and an unconventional shape.
- Design business cards in the shape of occupations, e.g. tennis coach, mortician, coat-hanger maker.
- Design and label an unusual invention to make cooking outdoors easier.

VARIATIONS AND FOLLOW-UP

- Link the object to be created with a current classroom topic, e.g. if you are working on mini-beasts, students can create a mini-beast zoo or a perfect butterfly house.
- Ask students to survey their parents and grandparents about the kinds of things they would like to see invented and why. Collate the data and make a poster of the results.
- Students can give group presentations on one of the following:
  - a great invention
  - a famous inventor
  - the rules of patenting and intellectual property.
- In groups of three, students can decide on the ten most significant inventions of the last 50 years. They should offer reasons for their choices.

Curator

A curator is the person who cares for, organises and oversees a collection or exhibition. Theme parks are one aspect of 'collections' and they are more than 'Disneyland'. There are small theme parks which are tourist attractions; there are exhibits which entertain and exhibits which educate. Some do both.

In this activity, students are required to plan and design theme parks or exhibits with specific features. The acronym THEME PARK CURATORS on Template 3 (see p 54) will give students assistance and direction.

Ideas to use

Provide each student with a copy of Template 3 (see p 54). Have students design a theme park, museum display or interactive exhibit around one of ideas listed below:

◊ rare minerals

ASPECT OF CREATIVITY
- Flexibility
- Creative problem-solving
- Originality
- Elaboration
- Logical thinking (logical application, deductive reasoning)

KLA FOCUS
- Health and Physical Education
- SOSE
- Science
- English
- Technology
- Mathematics
- LOTE
- Arts

AGE SUITABILITY
- Years 3–9

RESOURCES AND PREPARATION
- Discuss the role of a curator as one who protects and displays.
- Introduce the concept of theme parks and virtual museums. Link this to an excursion to a museum, or to the students' own experiences of theme parks and exhibits.

- fossils and animal scats (dung), e.g. a Poo-sorium
- pyrotechnics (fireworks)
- farm machinery
- jewellery (gold and silver smithing)
- perfumes and potions
- shoes, hats, veils and/or masks
- old crafts, e.g. rope-making, candle- and soap-making, blacksmithing
- orchards, e.g. fruit-picking, bottling, canning, sauces, wines, vinegars, diseases
- flight
- unusual inventions
- pioneers
- Sports Hall of Fame
- wool
- bushrangers
- insects
- clocks and time
- toys
- Egyptology
- dinosaurs
- toilets
- cartoons/animation
- heroes
- water
- sugar and honey
- lavender
- phones
- wood
- butterflies
- favourite cartoon show (or TV show)
- cats or dogs
- magazines
- fruit
- carrots
- humour.

VARIATIONS AND FOLLOW-UP

- Research the 'giant' objects which already exist, e.g. the Giant Pineapple, the Giant Sheep.
- Put together a photographic display of exhibits and theme parks from the students' experiences.
- Analyse theme parks which students have already visited to generate some working ideas.
- Students can draw plans, make models, create brochures, write descriptions, act as spruikers, etc.
- Students can make video/screen ads for their theme park or exhibit.
- Since tourists tend to visit theme parks, students can design an exhibit for people who do not speak the local language.

TEMPLATE 3

THEME PARKS

- **T**   Theme park's name and theme
- **H**   Health and safety concerns, e.g. first aid, danger
- **E**   Entry fee; Enormous 'giant' theme object/person
- **M**   Maps, e.g. 'You are here', printed maps; Multimedia displays, e.g. film, video, audiotaped guides, etc.
- **E**   Environments, i.e. buildings and grounds; Exhibits
- **P**   Plan of the park; Photographic opportunities; Playground; Picnic areas; Phones; Products to buy; Programs
- **A**   Activities to participate in; Assistance to visitors
- **R**   Rides; Research into the history
- **K**   Knowledge about the theme
- **C**   Carparking; Conveniences; Childminding; 'Characters' who dress up and wander around
- **U**   Undercover areas in case it rains
- **R**   Restaurant and food outlets (theme-related food)
- **A**   Advertising
- **T**   Tickets; Ticket sellers; Transport around the grounds
- **O**   Other languages
- **R**   Rides
- **S**   Staff; Signage; Souvenirs; Shops; Seating; Shows, e.g. displays and demonstrations; Smellovision

Designer

Fashion changes very rapidly and often tells us many things about the culture, the time period, the economy, etc. The following activity could follow a unit of work on fashion. Students are asked to creatively design unusual fashion items.

Designing ideas

Ask students to design, make, and/or put together original theme-related fashion items and accessories for a specific purpose. On completion of this activity, have students ask others for feedback. The students may wish to use some of the following ideas:

- a new Australian uniform for the next Olympics
- hats for a hat parade where personality or occupation is expressed in the choice of hat (optional commentary by compère)

ASPECT OF CREATIVITY
- Originality
- Imagination
- Flexibility
- Evaluation (road testing)

KLA FOCUS
- Arts
- Technology

AGE SUITABILITY
- Years 3–9

RESOURCES AND PREPARATION
- Various art and craft materials.

- masks for special occasions, e.g. rituals, camouflage and control (as in maintaining power)
- finalists' clothing for a 'Bad Taste Award'
- single-colour clothing
- eco-natural suits and outfits
- edible (fruit) jewellery
- newspaper cloaks
- 'a million-dollar look' (fake banknotes and coins as part of the design)
- personalised nails
- gloves with a medieval theme, e.g. 'Throwing down the gauntlet'
- hand-painted tights with maths formulaic themes
- op-shop chic – recycled clothing according to a decade, e.g. 1920s 'Flappers', 1970s 'Hippies'
- clothes with animal prints or skin patterns
- unusual sunglasses
- school bags with flair
- a floppy see-through sunhat for sports people
- an outfit for catching butterflies
- an outfit for a rock singer.

VARIATIONS AND FOLLOW-UP

- Have a fashion parade and film it.
- Display photographs of the designs. Add captions.
- Interview student designers.
- Research a decade (or a 25-year period) in history in relation to fashion. What do the clothes of the time tell you about other aspects of the culture and economy?
- Why does fashion change? Put forward a hypothesis and rationale.

Devil's advocate

Being able to argue logically for a point of view that you may not hold, is a useful skill. This activity asks students to argue for an absurd proposition which challenges traditional assumptions but which, nonetheless, has some merit. The creative aspect comes from the selection of key points and how they are presented.

Absurd propositions

Students select one (or more) of the following absurd propositions and argue convincingly in favour of it (they can use props) e.g. counter the idea that every person should take a day off for every celebration worldwide (holy days, independence days, birthdays of significant people, etc.), by arguing that the calendar is too full for anyone to work at all. A calendar, marked with all possible holidays, could be used as a prop. Invite students to choose one of the following absurd propositions and defend it.

ASPECT OF CREATIVITY
- Logical thinking (deductive reasoning, hypothetical thinking)
- Flexibility

KLA FOCUS
- English

AGE SUITABILITY
- Years 5–9

RESOURCES AND PREPARATION
- Discuss the concept of 'playing the devil's advocate' which means deliberately being provocative by taking the opposing point of view, in order test a proposition. It is an intellectual exercise and one does not have to believe the point of view that is being proposed.

- In order to reduce stress, there should be no clocks or watches.
- People with red hair have superior abilities to those with dark, blond or no hair.
- Each child should have three 'parents'.
- Birthdays should be abolished to save time.
- Days of the week should be colour-coded, e.g. students wear only red clothes and eat red food on 'Red Day'.
- Each of us should be responsible for three dependents (people, animals or plants).
- Money should be replaced by a barter system.
- Progressive replacement of the letter 'e' must happen because it is vital to the economy.
- Only people of exactly the same height may live together.
- Each person should only be permitted to walk ten kilometres a day.
- Every household should have at least one elderly person to look after.
- Every child should have their own horse.
- Because males are involved in more traffic accidents, more crime and look after their health less, they should pay more tax.

VARIATIONS AND FOLLOW UP

- Research how the role of 'devil's advocate' is used in the Catholic Church.
- Where might it be useful to play the role of 'devil's advocate' in order to point out the gaps and flaws in a position, e.g. a lawyer might do this with a client before a case.
- Conduct a mock trial (with a judge, jury, prosecuting lawyer and defence lawyer) of an individual related to a current topic, e.g. if you are focusing on environmental issues, try:
  ~ a logger
  ~ a 'greenie'

- an eco-terrorist (who, for example, rams whaling ships)
- someone who doesn't recycle.

e.g. if you are working on the topic of animals, try:

- the manager of a company who uses animals in cosmetic experiments
- the owner of a circus
- the owner/rescuer of 20 formerly stray cats who annoys her neighbours.

Different endings

Planning an appropriate ending which fits the rest of a story, song or film, but which goes in a different direction, requires both creative thinking and logical structuring. In this activity, students are asked to rewrite established stories, songs, poems, plays, jokes and scripts with an original, but not ridiculous, ending. They must state their rationale for the new ending and the source of the original material.

This is an advanced form of creative writing because to complete this activity successfully, students need a sound understanding of the original material's genre.

Rewriting ideas

You can offer students the structured options below or they can select their own songs, stories, plays, poems, jokes, films, videos and TV shows. They should be able to state key points about the style and the main features of the original material, in order to justify their new ending.

ASPECT OF CREATIVITY
- Flexibility
- Elaboration
- Originality
- Evaluation (road testing)
- Logical thinking

KLA FOCUS
- English
- Music
- Technology

AGE SUITABILITY
- Years 3–12

RESOURCES AND PREPARATION
- Demonstrate the process using a sample song or story.

Songs

Students choose and then rewrite the last few lines of self-selected songs or use well-known specified songs. The following are starting suggestions:

- the National Anthem
- 'Waltzing Matilda'
- sports club songs
- very well-known pop songs.

Stories, plays and poems

Students can select from the following list:

- myths and legends
- fairytales
- classic poems, stories or plays such as Gulliver's Travels, Moby Dick, The Importance of Being Earnest, Romeo and Juliet, The Man from Snowy River
- their personal favourites
- classic children's picture books.

Jokes

Students can select from the following list:

- the Internet
- joke books
- newspaper cartoons.

Films, videos and TV shows

Students can select from the following list:

- favourite films, videos and TV shows
- very well-known films, videos and TV shows.

VARIATIONS AND FOLLOW-UP

- Students swap and evaluate each other's new endings using a criteria grid (see an example on p 8) and the criteria of:
  - logic (1–10)
  - soundness of the rationale (1–10)
  - appeal (1–10).

- Read students a short story but stop before the ending is revealed. In groups of three, have students develop a suitable conclusion. Compare each group's ending to the original. This can also be done with a TV show episode, play script, film, joke or poem.

Experiments and surveys

There is a great deal of creativity required in deciding what to research, the scope of the research and how best to research a particular question. In this activity, students plan experiments and surveys to answer unusual questions which they are given.

Ideas for experiments and surveys

Students design an experiment or survey to test an interesting and unusual hypothesis. They can also, in some cases, carry it out and write a report.

- ◊ Humans assume that birds can't count, but that they can estimate groups. Wary of danger, birds fly away from a tower when a person enters at the bottom door. They stay away until the person comes out. If two people go in, the birds wait until two come out. The same with three. But if four people go in and three come out, the birds think it is safe, and they return. So, it is claimed that they

ASPECT OF CREATIVITY
- Creative problem-solving
- Logical thinking (hypothetical thinking, deductive reasoning)

KLA FOCUS
- Mathematics
- Science

AGE SUITABIlITY
- Years 3–9

RESOURCES AND PREPARATION
- Discuss the concept of a hypothesis, a survey, an experiment and controlling other factors apart from the one being investigated.

'group' rather than count. Devise an experiment which will test 'bird maths' and whether they can count. Ask, 'What am I testing? What will I use as subjects?' Write a report on your experiment. How will the results be presented?

- Design an experiment to test whether people obey 'DO NOT WALK ON THE GRASS' signs. What if they skip or dance instead?
- Design an experiment to test whether dogs (or cats) understand commands or just the tone in which they are given (use at least two languages).
- Design an experiment to test whether it's possible to hear a whispered conversation in a boat mid-lake, from the water's edge.
- Design an experiment to test whether dolphins are altruistic.
- Design an experiment to test how much time people spend in specific parts of the school.
- Design an experiment to investigate what are the most popular library books.
- Design an experiment or survey to investigate the most popular ice-cream flavours.
- Design an experiment to investigate how people behave in lifts and on escalators/travelators.

VARIATIONS AND FOLLOW-UP

- Across a reasonably long period of time, students can collect articles which describe unusual research studies, e.g. studies on what smells men and women prefer, increased water usage during TV commercial times (toilet flushing).
- As a class, discuss and list all the interesting questions people have about the behaviour of people and animals.
- Students can use the 'vox populi' strategy (interviewing people on the street, at random). Using a recorder, they interview people about the questions they would like researched. Data can be collated and graphed.

Frankenstein

We called this topic 'Frankenstein' because it involves putting together lots of different bits and pieces to creatively produce a new product just as the author, Mary Shelley, did with her monster). We have included some unusual 'bits' to encourage curiosity and challenge students' research skills. Students are asked to research unusual items, concepts and games, and then put together three 'bits' from these different items, concepts and games to form one new one.

'Frankenstein' selections

Allow students to choose any three of the following items, concepts and games to put together.

Alternatively, write out the choices on cards, and have them 'dip in' and select three. All of the three selections must be used in some way.

ASPECT OF CREATIVITY
- Imagination
- Elaboration
- Synectics
- Curiosity
- Logical reasoning (logical application)

KLA FOCUS
- English
- SOSE
- Health and Physical Education
- Music
- Science
- Mathematics
- Arts

AGE SUITABILITY
- Years 3–9

RESOURCES AND PREPARATION
- This activity features many unusual items, concepts or games and these will need to be researched in advance.

Animal

Create a new animal using selected parts and features from three of the following animals. Give your new animal a name. Describe what it can do. Draw it in colour.

- elephant
- giraffe
- platypus
- wart-hog
- panther
- caribou
- dodo
- unicorn
- bunyip

Team sport

Create a new team sport which incorporates elements from any three of the following sports. Give your new sport a name. Create a plan to advertise it. Describe how to play it. Draw the resources needed.

- hockey
- cricket
- soccer
- basketball
- netball
- baseball
- water polo
- Australian Rules Football
- vigoro
- volleyball
- walking football
- wheelchair basketball

Sporting pastime

Create a new individual sporting pastime which incorporates elements from any three of the following pastimes. Give your new game a name. Describe how it is played. Create a company to market it and devise a marketing strategy.

- roller blading
- swimming
- aerobics
- bushwalking
- orienteering or rogaining
- weight-lifting
- jet-skiing
- snow-skiing
- water-skiing
- ice-skating
- cycling
- kite-flying
- triathlon
- kayaking
- skydiving
- hang-gliding
- archery
- hopscotch

Partner sport

Create a new sport which needs at least two participants, and which incorporates elements from any three of the following sports. Give your new sport a name. Describe how to play it. Design suitable clothing. Outline the rules and draw the equipment needed.

- tennis
- squash
- table tennis
- snooker
- badminton
- rowing
- pètanque
- croquet
- royal tennis

Plant

Create a new plant or tree which incorporates elements from any three of the following plants and trees. Name your new plant. Draw it in full bloom. What other uses does it have?

- rose
- jasmine
- eucalypt
- orange tree
- pine tree
- rubber tree
- ivy
- grapevine
- Venus flytrap
- blackberry
- oleander
- poppy
- acacia

Philosophy

Create a new philosophy which incorporates elements from any three of the following philosophies. Name your new philosophy. Outline the beliefs.

What kind of people will this philosophy attract?

- Buddhism
- Christianity
- Islam
- Taoism
- Seventh Day Adventism
- Judaism
- Jehovah's Witness
- nihilism
- existentialism
- agnosticism
- communism
- democracy

Kitchen utensil

Create a new kitchen utensil which incorporates elements from any three of the following utensils. Name your new implement. Draw and advertise it.

- whisk
- food processor
- tongs
- knife
- hand-held mixer
- can opener
- peeler
- spatula
- spaghetti server
- carving fork
- corkscrew
- turkey baster
- vacuum pump
- vegetable scrubber
- mincer

Form of transport

Create a new form of transport which incorporates elements from any three of the following forms. Name your new transport and draw it.

- helicopter
- submarine
- horse and cart
- skateboard
- wheelchair
- bicycle
- glider
- ski
- kayak
- caravan
- bus
- motorcycle with a sidecar
- hearse
- pram
- removal van
- hansom cab
- taxi

Food

Create a new food which incorporates elements from any three of the following foods. Name your new food. Estimate its nutritional value. Draw and advertise it.

- quiche
- cheese stick
- pie
- battered fish
- crêpe
- pasta
- risotto
- drop scone

- sandwich
- Irish stew
- Pizza
- toad-in-the-hole
- dim sim
- spotted dog
- sausage roll
- bread and butter pudding
- scone
- black pudding
- pikelet
- haggis
- sponge cake
- escargot
- dried fruit strip
- casserole

Item of furniture

Create a new item of furniture which incorporates elements from any three of the following items. Name your new furniture. Draw it and describe its uses.

- commode
- stool
- chest of drawers
- rocking chair
- a desk
- secretaire
- four-poster bed
- hat stand
- umbrella stand
- throne
- prayer stool

TV show

Create a new TV show which incorporates elements from any three of the following kinds of TV shows. Name and describe your new show. Outline the kind of audience it would attract. Allocate a time slot for it and list advertisers who might sponsor the show.

- news
- current affairs program
- lifestyle program
- quiz show
- wildlife documentary
- 'The making of…' documentary
- interview program
- music show
- sports panel show

Magazine

Create a new magazine which incorporates elements from any three current magazines and/or newspapers. Name your new magazine. What is the target readership?

Toy

Create a new toy which incorporates elements from any three of the following toys. Name and draw your new toy.

- model railway set
- yo-yo
- doll
- matchbox car
- super bouncing ball
- doll's house
- hoop and stick
- rocking horse
- pick-up-sticks
- spinning top
- kite
- marbles

Playground equipment

Create a new piece of playground equipment which incorporates elements from any three of the following pieces of equipment. Name your new equipment. Draw and describe it.

- swing
- slide
- flying fox
- monkey bars
- jungle gym
- seesaw
- tunnel
- sandpit
- merry-go-round
- trampoline
- jumping castle

Item of clothing

Create a new item of clothing which incorporates elements from any three of the following pieces of clothing. Name and draw your new clothing. List its advantages and disadvantages.

- cardigan
- cloak
- top hat
- flares
- scarf
- dancing slippers
- long buttoned gloves
- veil
- harem pants
- corset
- waistcoat
- jeans
- pumps
- tuxedo
- kilt
- camisole
- cravat
- stays
- cape

Insect or mini-beast

Create a new insect or mini-beast which incorporates elements from any three of the following insects and mini-beasts. Name your new creature. Draw it. What role does it play in nature?

- locust
- red back spider
- ant
- cicada
- Christmas beetle
- dung/scarab beetle
- frog
- cane toad
- slater
- black widow spider
- leech
- silverfish
- termite

Tool

Create a new tool which incorporates elements from any three of the following tools. Name and draw your new tool. What can it be used for? What safety features will you need to add? Create a campaign to persuade hardware stores to stock it.

- axe
- screwdriver
- claw hammer
- awl
- saw
- anvil
- router

Illness

Create a new illness which incorporates elements from any three of the following sicknesses. Name your new illness. Create a campaign to convince the government to allocate money to find a cure.

- measles
- blackwater fever
- tuberculosis
- mumps
- scarlet fever
- leprosy
- cholera
- dengue fever
- whooping cough
- malaria
- black plague

Electrical gadget

Create a new piece of electrical equipment which incorporates elements from any three of the following gadgets. Name your new piece of equipment.

Draw and label it. Decide on an advertising campaign aimed at a specific group of consumers.

- carving knife
- vertical grill
- hair dryer with a hood
- bread baker
- crêpe maker
- hand-held beater
- drill
- hand-held vacuum cleaner
- answering machine
- modem

Building

Create a new building which incorporates elements from any three of the following structures. Draw your new structure.

- vestibule
- parlour
- foyer
- pantry
- passageway
- loft
- bathroom
- attic
- outhouse
- cellar
- conservatory
- anteroom
- sunroom
- scullery
- gazebo
- pergola
- boiler room
- chamber
- entrance hall
- staircase
- balcony
- veranda
- mezzanine
- patio
- courtyard
- pavilion

VARIATIONS AND FOLLOW-UP

- Students create some similar tasks for younger students in years K–1 involving pictures or photographs. Use junk mail catalogues.
- Play the game whereby someone draws a head and then folds the paper over. They then pass it on to another class member. The next person draws the chest and arms, the third person adds the legs

and the rest of the trunk, the fourth person adds the feet, and the fifth person looks at the whole 'person' and names it. Name the game, e.g. Heads Down?

- Students give a brief presentation on an unusual item they have researched.
- Students can research and present a report on Frankenstein and/or other similar 'put together' fictional monsters.
- Link this activity with cloning, genetic engineering, cross-fertilisation, grafting of plants and trees, and cross-species breeding.

Graphic stories

Interpreting a graph requires logic and an understanding of graphing conventions. However, there can also be a creative aspect to interpreting a graph as the reason for a change in the line or curve is not always obvious. In this activity, students are asked to build stories around graphs which explain their changes in a creative but realistic manner. Students then make up their own graph to interpret or for others to interpret. Two graphs have been provided. However, lots of other ideas for students to use when creating graphs are listed.

Students look closely at the graphic clues and then write down a list of facts, e.g. at 8 am there was no water, at 9 am the pool filled to two metres, etc. They then use two columns and list things that might have made the water go up and things that might have made the level go down. For example:

- an elephant peed in the pool
- they filled it up with a hose

ASPECT OF CREATIVITY
- Originality
- Logical thinking (deductive reasoning)
- Flexibility
- Imagination

KLA FOCUS
- Mathematics
- English
- Technology

AGE SUITABILITY
- Years 4–12

RESOURCES AND PREPARATION
- Graph paper and familiarity with the concept of co-ordinates.

- more bodies in the pool displaced the water (a geriatric aqua-aerobics class with lots of heavy people)
- the water temporarily froze over (ice expands)
- the local fire brigade used the water for an emergency bushfire
- water bombing by children
- a circus elephant used its trunk to drain the pool
- the pool was partially emptied by maintenance workers for repainting
- the pool was drained due to a pool infection scare.

Example A: Country Town Swimming Pool water levels

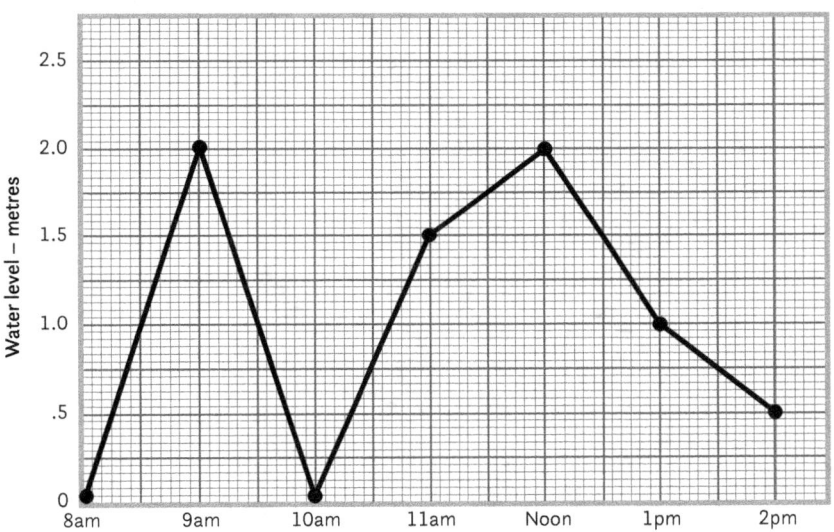

Question: Why does the water level change over six hours?

The storyteller has to link some of these suggestions together in a believable way. The following is an example of a story based on the graph in Example A.

> This summer, the Country Town Swimming Pool had a problem. The pool was empty one morning at 8 am but suddenly rose to 2m by 9 am. A rumour grew that a straying

elephant from the nearby circus had peed in the pool. Despite the heat, locals didn't want to swim there. Then several swimmers, who couldn't resist plunging in, complained of eye infections, so the management drained the pool (down to 0), painted the pool floor red, white and blue, and then refilled it (up to 1.5m). Lap swimmers returned, and so did the daily geriatric aqua aerobics and SCUBA class. The water level went up (up to 2m) due to the numbers involved. During the midday heat, a bushfire broke out and the local fire brigade pumped out pool water to save houses and the circus tents (down to 1m). The elephant helped by sucking water with his trunk and spraying it on spot fires (down to .5m). The locals started a new rumour about the fire brigade having an elephant as a mascot.

Example B: People in the park

Write a story to explain this graph.

Writing your own graphic story

Students choose one variable to go on each axis of the graph. They need to use things which can be measured, and which increase and decrease over time. The following ideas can be used by students:

- temperatures in a house over 24 hours
- number of people in a park over six hours
- number of living things in the kitchen from 7 am to midnight
- amount of money in a bank account over a week
- amount of pocket money in the bank between mid-December and the end of January
- noise level (in decibels) in a city square (rock-and-roll band, siren, last bus leaves, spruiker, etc.)
- amount of money thrown into a charity wishing well
- heart rate of adventurous dog (if you plot one point as zero, does this mean the dog is dead or that the heart monitor has stopped?).

VARIATIONS AND FOLLOW-UP

- Students can plot their own story on graph paper and then swap. Their partner works out a story based on the points and thinks of a title.
- Use continuous cooperative stories. Working in groups of five, each student creates their own five-point graph. These are then passed around the group. One person explains only one point, and then passes the story on. All contribute to the five stories, finishing their own with a twist.
- Students can draw the graphs using computer graphics.
- Try this activity in reverse. Give students a story containing increases and decreases which they then graph, e.g. a story about pulse rates and emotions.

How many can you think of?

In this activity, students list as many things as they can which fit a stated criterion, e.g. list all the things you can think of which are black and white. The skill of brainstorming (see p 4) is the first step in the creative process. The more effective and creative ideas usually come later in the sequence of brainstormed ideas. To increase students' understanding of the concept of 'originality' they are given bonus points for each item they list which no other student pair has thought of. Systematic Alphabetic Generation (SAG – see p 4) is used as a tool for brainstorming.

Criteria

In pairs, give students a stated criterion or several criteria, e.g. soft and yellow, and ask them how many things they can think of which fit this description. Each pair then reads out their list. As each list is read, other students raise their hands if they also have that idea. (Make sure students do not continue to read those ideas that have

ASPECT OF CREATIVITY
- Fluency (listing, Systematic Alphabetic Generation)
- Originality

KLA FOCUS
- English
- Science
- Arts
- Mathematics
- Music
- SOSE
- LOTE
- Health and Physical Education

AGE SUITABILITY
- Years 3–9

RESOURCES AND PREPARATION
- Teach Systematic Alphabetic Generation first (see p 4).

already been stated.) Students receive one point for each accurate idea and an extra five points for any idea on their list which no-one else had thought of. Ask the students how many things they can think of that fit the following criteria:

- soft and yellow
- bounces
- changes temperature a lot during the day
- could be used to measure how tall you are
- goes green
- can fit in a matchbox
- rolls
- triangular or pyramid-shaped
- made from potato
- includes a magnifying glass
- has a button to push in
- reversible
- includes a light bulb
- framed
- has a speaker
- includes information about the current date
- has more than one handle
- has a cork
- has wings
- sleeps more than wakes
- has an ID tag
- wrapped in cellophane
- costs less than 20 cents
- frequently lost by people
- could balance on an apple without falling off
- words that end with '-cide' or '-ky'
- words that rhyme with 'fusion'
- words that contain double consonants
- words that contain the letter group 'ert'
- words that start with 'anti-' or 'ante-'.

VARIATIONS AND FOLLOW-UP

- ◊ Students create their own categories for class use in relation to specific topics. For example:
    - ~ if you are focusing on measurement, students might come up with the question, 'How many things can you think of which have a ruler built in?'
    - ~ if you are dealing with the sea, students could ask, 'How many kinds of marine life can you think of which have an attacking method of defending themselves? or 'How many things can you think of which are amphibious?'
    - ~ if you are completing a topic on recreation and leisure, students could come up with the question, 'How many sports can you think of which don't use a ball?'

How many ways?

Being able to adapt your mind to novel ways of seeing a familiar item or situation is an important aspect of creative thinking. In this activity, students identify as many unusual uses for a stated item or as many ways to tackle a problem as they can.
The emphasis is on both brainstorming and adaptability. To increase students' understanding of the concept of 'originality' they are then asked to select two of the things on their list which they believe that no-one else will have thought of. If they are correct, they receive bonus points. This is different to the previous activity (see p 78) where students were given bonus points for all unique answers. Here they have to predict which two of their answers might be unique. This encourages them to discriminate the 'typical' from the 'unusual'. Systematic Alphabetic Generation (SAG – see p 4) is used as a tool for brainstorming.

ASPECT OF CREATIVITY
- Fluency (listing, Systematic Alphabetic Generation, brainstorming)
- Originality
- Flexibility

KLA FOCUS
- English
- Science
- Arts
- Mathematics
- Music
- SOSE
- LOTE
- Health and Physical Education

AGE SUITABILITY
- Years 3–9

RESOURCES AND PREPARATION
- Where possible, bring the item into the classroom.
- Teach Systematic Alphabetic Generation (see p 4).

What to do

Students work with a partner to identify ways to use an unusual item or solve a simple problem. Students then select two of their ideas which they believe no-one else will have thought of. Each pair then reads out their list and states the two ideas they think are unique. If another student pair has either of the two ideas on their list, they raise their hands. The pair gets one point for each acceptable idea and an extra ten points for each selected unique idea, which did in fact, turn out to be unique. Ask groups not to repeat ideas already stated. Ask students how many ways they can think of to use the following items (students can bring objects from home to use with this task):

- coat-hanger
- pair of goggles
- odd socks
- stepladder
- used Christmas or birthday cards
- a sheet of tissue paper
- three paper clips
- name tags
- discarded spectacles
- empty milk cartons.

Ask the students how many ways to solve the following problems.

- stop students from throwing litter in the playground
- remove graffiti
- create an edible '13 shape' to go on a birthday cake
- take the smell out of track shoes
- stop the sound of a tap dripping
- design a safety warning for blind people
- toddler-proof a kitchen to make it safe
- get a person up on time in the morning
- stop snails eating mail in the letter box
- clean windows without leaving a smear
- stop hiccups.

VARIATIONS AND FOLLOW-UP

◇ Students create their own questions for class use in relation to specific topics. For example:
  - if you are focusing on measurement, students might come up with the question, 'How many ways can you find to weigh your pet?'
  - if you are dealing with government, students could ask, 'How many ways could you tax reading/laughter/arguments/dogs who leave droppings/lost property?'
  - if you are working on health, students might ask, 'How many ways could you deliver vaccination programs cheaply and conveniently to parents?'

Jeopardy

Knowing the answer to a question requires knowledge and memory. Knowing how to reverse the sequence and work out what the question might have been when you are only given the answer, requires more flexible thinking.

Generating a range of possible questions which could lead to the same answer requires creative and logical thinking. Give simple statements or single words and ask students to think of as many unusual questions as they can for which the word or statement could be an accurate answer. The emphasis is not on finding the one correct factual question, but rather on identifying as many question options as possible.

This activity is named after a popular, long-running American TV show.

If the answer is 'green and blue', what might the question be?

Questions could be:

- ◇ What are two popular colours?
- ◇ What are the colours of the sea?

ASPECT OF CREATIVITY
- Flexibility
- Originality
- Logical thinking (deductive reasoning, logical application)
- Fluency (brainstorming)

KLA FOCUS
- English
- Science
- Arts
- Mathematics
- Music
- SOSE
- LOTE
- Health and Physical Education

AGE SUITABILITY
- Years 3–9

RESOURCES AND PREPARATION
- Model the process. Repeatedly stress that you are looking for more than just one simple, correct, factual question.

- What is a colour for jealousy and another for sadness?
- What are common eye colours?
- What is 'eulb' and 'neerg' in reverse?

If the answer is 'a hot fridge', what might the question be?

Questions could be:

- What happens when you cross a microwave oven with a fridge?
- What happens during a power cut?
- What's another name for a stolen cooler?

Answers to use as 'starters'

- a ripe tomato
- a green triangle
- a key ring
- a peacock feather
- gold lettering
- because they have no buttons
- ten dollars but it varies
- H2O
- a stapler
- a burnt sausage
- a flag
- black and green

VARIATIONS AND FOLLOW-UP

- Ask each group of students to generate answers for another group and in turn, provide questions for that group's answers.
- Place the 'answer' on a bulletin board and invite students to provide questions over a week.

- Set up a 'Jeopardy Bank' with a 'answer box' in which students deposit ten copies of one answer. Other students can 'withdraw' an answer and make up questions for it and deposit these in a 'question box'.
- Students can research the meaning of 'jeopardy' and find as many synonyms as they can. They can also discuss why the TV game is called 'Jeopardy'.
- Students can research the concept of 'double jeopardy' and discuss how it could be used as a plot device in a story.

Landscaping

Very little about landscaping is tackled in schools, and yet it is a fascinating area which will be relevant to many students' adult life. Planning and designing your personal outdoor space is an important life skill. In this activity, students plan, design, build models of, or plant gardens or environments to fit specified criteria.

What to do

Ask students to draw plans or make models of a specific landscape (garden). In their plan or model, students are asked to specify distances, numbers, volumes and lengths. Ask them to list the necessary components, and the quantities required, e.g. soil, light, water, nutrients.

Types of gardens to design

- a display garden at the Olympic Games
- a highly scented garden with a fountain or waterfall feature

ASPECT OF CREATIVITY
- Logical application (reasoning)
- Originality
- Evaluation (road testing)

KLA FOCUS
- Science
- Mathematics
- Arts
- Technology

AGE SUITABILITY
- Years 4–12

RESOURCES AND PREPARATION
- Show photos of gardens.
- Bring in photos of your favourite spots (home or public gardens).

- an anti-insect garden, e.g. anti-mosquito
- a collection of pot plants which contain trailing highly coloured plants, plus two pots which feature exotic ferns
- a collection of hanging baskets which offer a three-colour theme and contrasting heights
- a mini garden of red flowers or shrubs only
- a 'smelly' scented herb garden where it will be easy for a blind person to find particular plants
- a vegetable garden which provides food all year (this may be in window boxes or pot plants)
- a bonsai garden or a Japanese garden
- a healing garden
- a hydroponics garden
- a window box for a high-rise apartment or boat
- an organic garden
- an underwater garden
- a symbiotic garden (where some plants rely on a symbiotic relationship with others)
- a children's 'play' garden
- a 'fast-growing' garden.

VARIATIONS AND FOLLOW-UP

- Students can design a 'how-to-care-for-me' booklet for their garden.
- Students can grow and maintain their garden.
- Students can use computer graphics to design and plan their garden.
- Interesting landscaping features or gardens can be photographed for a display.

Links

Being able to find ways in which two or three unrelated things are similar and bring them together requires flexible thinking. Flexible thinking increases the likelihood of seeing unusual connections which can result in a novel outcome. To increase students' understanding of the concept of 'originality', they are given bonus points for each link they list which no other pair has thought of. This kind of thinking also leads to an understanding of similes, metaphors and analogies.

How are a 'teacher' and an 'elephant' alike?

- Both have long memories.
- Both have two 'e's' and an 'a' in their names.
- Both sometimes give others a 'spray'.
- They both seem awfully large and impressive when you first meet them!

What to do

In groups of three, have students identify ways in which two seemingly unrelated items are the same, and/or identify ways in

ASPECT OF CREATIVITY
- Flexibility
- Originality
- Logical thiking (analogical thinking)
- Synectics
- Fluency (listing attributes)

KLA FOCUS
- English
- Science
- Arts
- Mathematics
- Music
- SOSE
- LOTE
- Health and Physical Education

AGE SUITABILITY
- Years 2–12

RESOURCES AND PREPARATION
- Model the process using two objects.

which two unrelated items can be used together. Start by listing all the attributes of both items. Pairs take turns to read out their lists. As each list is read out, other pairs raise their hands if they also have that link. (Ask groups not to read out links which have already been stated.) Pairs receive one point for each accurate fit and an extra five points for any links on their list which no-one else has thought of.

Link starters

How are these two things alike?

- an umbrella and a map
- a street directory and a coin
- a traffic light and a lemon tart
- a quilt and a window
- soap and a lemon
- a screwdriver and a hot-air balloon
- a magazine and a teaspoon

As an extra task, ask students to find a way in which the two items or people could be used together.

Another way to link

In groups of three, students compile a list of ten things. They then write each item on a card or a piece of paper. All cards are put into a container and a representative from each group pulls out two cards.

VARIATIONS AND FOLLOW-UP

- Students could use three items instead of two.
- Use real objects.
- Students can propose ideas for similar tasks or bring in objects or photos.
- Younger students can use pictures from catalogues as props.

Lucky dip

The skill of creatively putting together random information and using it productively to tell a feasible story, is a high-level writing skill. But the following three versions of the 'lucky dip' activity are also fun!

From a container, students 'dip in' and draw out cards containing unrelated pieces of information. They then build oral or written stories or scripts around what they read on the cards.

Version 1: Using word cues

In pairs, students prepare and perform an oral story using the clue they drew in at least three different ways, e.g. the clue card might say 'key', but it could be used in the oral story as 'door key', 'car key', 'khaki', 'keyboard', 'monkey', 'donkey', 'quay', 'key card'. This strategy also develops an understanding of homonyms and multiple meanings.

ASPECT OF CREATIVITY
- Originality
- Synectics
- Flexibility
- Evaluation (road testing)

KLA FOCUS
- English

AGE SUITABILITY
- Years K–12

RESOURCES AND PREPARATION
- Make story card containers (bag, box or chest).
- Blank cards.

The following are starter words which could be used as clues:

- net (fish-net, fishing net, Internet, network, hair net)
- fork (fork in the road, pitch-fork, eating implement, fork in a tree)
- ball (dance, toy, game)
- ring (sound, worn on hand, circle, ring of spies)
- counter (person who counts, shop bench, used in a board game or personal exercise).

Version 2: Story endings

A story ending can also be 'lucky-dipped'. Students are asked to create a story which ends with one of the following phrases:

- At last, the trapdoor closed.
- The ghost was really a possum.
- The khaki car key was displayed at the show.
- Supermarket trolleys need learner-driver plates.
- It wasn't really cheese at all.
- And the gnome was left out on the lawn until the next rubbish collection.
- Luckily, at 18, you can change your name by deed poll.
- Well, now I'm stuck with it for the next year.
- Having no petrol didn't stop us in the end.

Version 3: Bits and pieces

Students take three cards from each of three different containers (labelled 'Character', 'Venue', 'Object') and build an oral story around these nine key pieces of information. The following are card ideas for each container.

Character

- caretaker of an unusual building
- sad clown
- accident-prone busker
- courier with poor navigation skills
- parking officer who wants to be liked
- nurse who has no patience

- volunteer fire brigade officer
- mayor in despair
- plumber who is claustrophobic
- bag lady
- angry animal trainer
- anxious bomb disposal expert
- someone who blushes a lot
- someone who giggles a lot
- someone who cries 'at the drop of a hat'
- marriage/name day celebrant
- pickpocket
- jockey
- person who writes greeting cards
- dog walker
- photographer
- personal trainer

Venue

- circus
- zoo
- grand final
- sleep laboratory
- up a tree
- graveyard
- TV studio
- bakery
- theme park
- dog obedience school
- racing track or BMX track
- skateboarding park with ramps
- kindergarten
- adventure playground
- 'outward bound' circuit
- Bass Strait oil rig (or ocean oil rig)
- aircraft/car simulator
- operating theatre

Object

- stopped escalator
- egg of a rare bird
- suitcase mistakenly collected
- heart monitor
- picnic basket
- footprint or voiceprint
- computer disk
- paintbrush
- credit card
- gold pen
- boomerang
- business card
- Bible

Version 4: titles

Students write stories after being given titles. For example:

- Green is Best
- Over the Top (Again!)
- Cushion Effect
- Bottles, But No Rice
- A Basket of Gloom
- Dancing King.

VARIATIONS AND FOLLOW-UP

- Alternatively, students can work in groups of three. One pulls out a character card, one a venue card and one an object card. They put these together to build an oral story. They then change groups but still keep their card. The new group of three make up another oral story with this new combination. Each new group could have one character, one venue and one object card, or topics could be unevenly distributed.
- Students can create their own clue words and story endings.

Mergers

This is a slightly more time-consuming activity than others in this book, but it is worth it! Realistically it could be performed across two weeks or even used as a creative theme for a term. Alternatively, it could be a one-session activity. Students merge two companies with very different products to come up with a new product which reflects the strengths of both. During this activity, there are many opportunities for artistic creativity as well.

Company names

The following is a list of companies for students to choose from:

- Nifty Noodles Inc.
- Just Hanging Around Flower Baskets
- Splat! Paint Company
- The Fertile Imagination Fertiliser Co.
- Keyhole Locksmiths
- Garden Gnomes Galore
- Countless Counting Supplies Inc.
- By Candle Light
- Kitty Litter Kingdom

ASPECT OF CREATIVITY
- Looking at the big picture (consider all factors, consider all the people)
- Consequential prediction
- Synectics
- Evaluation (criteria grid or road testing)
- Originality
- Flexibility

KLA FOCUS
- Technology
- Arts
- Science
- SOSE
- Mathematics

AGE SUITABILITY
- Years 5–9

RESOURCES AND PREPARATION
- Blank name tags.
- Blank pieces of cardboard the size of business cards.

- Roll On Bike Bits
- 'Bin It' Waste Bins Inc.
- H2O to Go
- Duplicate Copying Company
- 'Cool Messages' Fridge Magnets
- We Light Up Your Life Light Bulb Company
- Balloons R Us
- Just Tables Inc.
- Megabite Vegetarian Sandwich Company
- Bubble and Fizz Soft Drink Company
- Fabulous Fishtanks Inc.
- Knot Really Ties
- Stacks of Vacs
- Shu-laces Going Places
- Shouts for Sprouts
- Party On Party Supplies.

How to organise a merger

- Organise students into groups of three to form a company.
- Give each student within a group a number from 1 to 3.
  - Student 1 is called Adam.
  - Student 2 is called Ben.
  - Student 3 is called Carol.
- Provide each group with a copy of Template 4 (see p 99) and tell them the name of the company to which they have been allocated. Each group of three students is the Board of Directors and an equal partner in the company. Each director prepares and wears a name tag.
- Invite each group to discuss their company. Have them make up appropriate and realistic facts. They then fill in Template 4 (see p 99) regarding their three top-selling products, and their strengths and weaknesses. The group decides on a company logo and makes a business card for each company director.

- Now each group member temporarily forms another 'visiting' group with people from other companies. Each visiting group should contain one Adam, one Ben and one Carol. There should not be two people from the same company in a visiting group. This is best achieved by the following strategy:
    - ask all the Adams to stay put
    - tell all the Bens to move one group to the left
    - ask all the Carols to move one group to the right.

    This strategy won't work unless there is a clear 'left' and 'right' in the room arrangement. It works best when the groups are in a circle. Alternatively, if there are no more than six groups, you can have all the Adams meeting in one group, all the Bens in another and all the Carols in another.

- Each visitor introduces themselves, shows their business cards, and briefly shares information about their company's three best products and strengths. Each person has a maximum of one minute to talk. Use a whistle or another device to signal when it is the next person's turn to talk.
- All directors now return to their original company groups.
- There is a downturn in the economy! So there will have to be mergers. Tell each group which company they have to merge with. (Randomly pull out combinations of companies from a container.)
- Each group of three now becomes a new group of six. The task is to create one new product reflecting the strengths and products of both companies. Give the product a name. Who is your target buyer? Plan your advertising campaign. Create your new company name. What will be the selling price? List all the factors which must be considered. Discuss all the people who must be considered and on whom your product might have an impact.
- Each newly merged company now has to give a presentation to the whole class on their new product. Specialise, i.e. the Carols should focus on finance, the Bens should be the 'challengers' whose job it is to play 'devil's advocate' and say things like 'Wearing my challenger's hat, can I ask/point out …', etc. This must be done

respectfully and without put-downs. The Adams should be the 'note-takers' and 'main spokesperson'.

- Products are drawn, described and a poster or brochure is made to place on a bulletin board.
- Now the whole class, as individuals, fills in an evaluation sheet on each newly developed product (see Template 5 p 100). This data is collated. The company whose product gets the highest overall evaluation, receives the 'Small Business of the Year' award.
- Alternatively, use the evaluation criteria grid on Template 5 (see p 100) to evaluate the new product.

VARIATIONS AND FOLLOW-UP

- Students can create their own companies with original names to use with this activity.
- Students can do follow-up research on:
  - small businesses
  - mergers
  - boards of directors
  - awards for small businesses
  - government agencies set up to assist small businesses
  - payroll tax
  - courses for people wanting to start a small business
  - the role of the Minister for Small Business
  - statistics about small businesses
  - interviews with parents or members of the local community who run small businesses
  - service clubs such as Rotary, Lions, Soroptimists, etc.
- Use companies which provide services rather than sell products. For example:
  - See-through Window Cleaning
  - Kids on the Run Childcare Centre
  - Tree Medico.

TEMPLATE 4
COMPANY FACTS

What is the name of your company?
_____

List the three directors of your company.

1. _____
2. _____
3. _____

Describe the three most successful products made by your company (outlining the strongest selling part of each).

1. _____
   _____

2. _____
   _____

3. _____
   _____

4. _____
   _____

What are the strengths of your company and its products?
_____
_____
_____
_____

TEMPLATE 5

PRODUCT EVALUATION: VERSION 1

What is the name of the product you are evaluating?

What market would it appeal to?

Approximate price:

Is this price reasonable for the product? ○ Yes ○ No

Would you buy this product/service? ○ Yes ○ No ○ Not sure

Give this product an overall rating.

    1   2   3   4   5   6   7   8   9   10

  LOUSY   SUPER

Do you think the market, which the group is aiming for, will really buy this product? Rate your answer.

    1   2   3   4   5   6   7   8   9   10

  NO CHANCE   HIGHLY LIKELY

What are the strengths of this product?

PRODUCT EVALUATION: VERSION 2

Please note: selection criteria (1–10, with 10 being best)

Criteria	Product: Company:
Cost appropriateness – does it represent good value for money?	
Consumer appeal – does the product appeal to you?	
Feasibility – does it work as a product which would sell to others?	
Total score	

Off-beat

The newspapers are full of weird and wonderful off-beat stories which make great resources for encouraging creative thinking. Use these as described to stimulate creativity in a whole range of areas such as writing, acting, drawing, problem-solving and research. Captions, headings, subheadings and/or headlines can encapsulate 'off-beat' story ideas.

Off-beat starters

These activities are based on off-beat news items. Students use the item as the basis of a story and/or use the follow-up questions/tasks.

Poor pigeons

Some workers in South African gold and diamond mines have been using carrier pigeons, smuggled in their lunch boxes, to fly out gems. They attach the gems to the birds and set them free. Mine owners have decided to shoot any pigeons in the area. The local pigeon club is upset but has agreed to cooperate.

ASPECT OF CREATIVITY
- Curiosity
- Flexibility
- Originality

KLA FOCUS
- English

AGE SUITABILITY
- Years 4–12

RESOURCES AND PREPARATION
- Various newspapers.

- Write a script around this news item (audio, screen or classroom performance).
- In a group of three, develop and perform a mock trial of a pigeon. Have a prosecutor, a defence lawyer and a judge.
- How could airspace above the mine be declared off-limits and patrolled?
- What possible legal difficulties could arise if an innocent bird is shot?
- Argue persuasively that the birds are more important than the gems.
- What else could the mining company do to solve their problem?
- Research the uses of carrier pigeons.

A flying cat

A cat disappeared from its travel cage in-flight on a Boeing 747. It was in transit between the east and west coasts. The cat ended up making several east-west-east trips because it took a long time to locate.

When the distraught owner was given permission to search the storage hold of the plane, the cat was found.

- Write a humorous story around this news item.
- Would the cat receive frequent flyer points? Where might it want to fly to in order to use them up and why, e.g. Kathmandu, the San Diego Zoo to see the big cats?
- Who should pay for its many flights?
- What are the rules regarding animal transport and quarantine in Australia? Are they fair?
- What problems could you encounter getting your pet to another state by plane and relocating it to its new home?
- List all the ways you can think of to identify a cat, e.g. a passport, a tattoo, miaow-prints.
- How could a cat get lost in a Boeing 747? Draw a diagram to illustrate your idea.
- What is the law regarding stowaways? What happens when they are found?

Lyrebird give-away

Lyrebirds are excellent mimics. After an arsonist deliberately started a fire in a national park, police used a lyrebird in an attempt to solve the crime of arson. A nearby lyrebird was making a sound very similar to that of a motorbike. Police suspected that the arsonist had driven away on such a vehicle. The earlier repertoire of the bird (who was known affectionately by locals as Henry) included bush noises, people, traffic and electronic game-boys, but hadn't previously included a motorbike. He also added to his repertoire the sound of the helicopters dumping water on the fire!

- Write a mystery story where a bird's ability to mimic is a key feature.
- Which birds can mimic and why?
- What are the unique characteristics of a lyrebird?

VARIATIONS AND FOLLOW-UP

- Ask students to collect their own off-beat newspaper cuttings to swap as the basis for further stories. They can also develop follow-up questions and/or tasks around them. Create a display board and appoint a caretaker.
- Students can discuss what makes a story 'off-beat' and list criteria.
- Students can problem-solve and research the question of how reporters find out about these off-beat stories.
- Inform students that they are journalists for a rural newspaper. Present them with a 'lead' about a polluted swamp where locals often swim, picnic and fish. However, tests have shown that the water seems to make people forgetful. Ask, 'How would you go about checking the facts, deciding on a story angle and thinking of a title?'

Picture this!

This is an enjoyable activity for encouraging artistic creativity. Students are asked to draw common idiomatic sayings in a literal way. They then turn them into posters, fridge magnets, etc. This exercise links in well with language activities.

Idiomatic sayings

Students select three of the following sayings and draw them:

- a ratbag
- a stone's throw away
- adding fuel to the fire
- all over the place like a
- dog's dinner
- an apple turnover
- as close as two peas in a pod
- as happy as a dog with two tails
- balancing the books
- beating around the bush
- bending over backwards
- blackmail

ASPECT OF CREATIVITY
- Flexibility
- Originality

KLA FOCUS
- Arts
- English
- Technology

AGE SUITABILITY
- Years 4–12

RESOURCES AND PREPARATION
- Discuss the meanings of common sayings which have 'drawable' components.
- Coloured pens.
- Drawing paper.

- blew up
- blood is thicker than water
- blowing your own trumpet
- buzz off
- cabin fever
- calling it quits
- can't get one's head around the problem
- 'cheesed off'
- climbing the walls
- a bull in a China shop
- cried her eyes out
- crying over spilt milk
- don't get your knickers in a knot
- dragging your heels
- eating humble pie
- eats like a horse
- falling off the wagon
- head over heels in love
- hit the ceiling
- hitting the nail on the head
- jumping on the bandwagon
- laughed her head off
- living close to the edge
- lose your heart
- making mountains out of molehills
- nose is out of joint
- nose is up in the air
- opening a can of worms
- passing the buck
- pulling out all stops

- pushing your luck
- putting someone up on a pedestal
- putting your foot in your mouth
- raining cats and dogs
- running around in circles
- skinny as a rake
- skirting around the problem
- start the ball rolling
- swallowing your pride
- throwing your weight around
- time on your hands
- elbow grease.

VARIATIONS AND FOLLOW-UP

- Students can research similar phrases and sayings which can then be shared or redistributed.
- Put the students' drawings on a bulletin board and have other students guess the sayings.
- Students can make an alphabetical book of sayings.
- Special occasion cards (featuring drawn and written idiomatic sayings) can be made and used within the school community, e.g. for times when congratulations, not insults, are required.

PIN numbers

Remembering PIN numbers or passwords is a challenge for most of us, as we tend to have quite a few to remember. The usual methods, such as using birth dates and anniversary dates are open to exploitation. This activity requires students to creatively problem-solve the issue of remembering PIN (Personal Identification Number) numbers and other relevant data ranging from small numbers to large. This activity has very practical applications within the school and community, and stresses the relevance of originality and logic in everyday situations.

Challenges

Students are asked to work in pairs to come up with solutions to the following challenges.

⋄ Ask students to come up with personalised ways to remember three given PIN numbers (which are not

ASPECT OF CREATIVITY
- Originality
- Logical thinking (logical application, deductive reasoning)
- Evaluation (road testing)

KLA FOCUS
- Mathematics
- SOSE

AGE SUITABILITY
- Years 4–12

RESOURCES AND PREPARATION
- Discuss the concepts of PIN numbers and passwords, and their functions.

simply birth dates or house numbers) and an explanation of why these ways will work.

❖ Have students imagine that they have a client who is prepared to pay well for strategies that help them remember their PIN numbers of four different accounts.

Account A requires a three-digit number.

Account B requires a four-digit number.

Account C requires a five-digit number.

Account D requires a six-digit number.

Devise a secure way which will make it simple for the client to remember their PIN numbers, but difficult for anyone else to 'crack' the system.

❖ In case your client forgets their four-digit number, you can teach them to use a system whereby you take the day and month of their birthday, and then subtract the last two digits of the year in which they were born.

Birthday = 12 January 1980

PIN = 12 (date) + 01 (month) = 1201

now subtract the year (80): 1201 - 80 = 1121

Remember to include ways to remember the strategy if the number is forgotten. Do your strategies work? Trial them. Who will you select for your trial? How will you evaluate your strategy? Get feedback on:

~ user-friendliness
~ successful remembering
~ possible difficulties.

VARIATIONS AND FOLLOW-UP

- Students can interview bank personnel about security issues in relation to PIN numbers.
- Students can identify other kinds of memory tasks for which memorisation systems could be devised such as finding a car in a car park, remembering a shopping list without actually taking it, etc.
- Follow up with mnemonic (memory strategies) tasks and memory games such as Concentration.

Plotting

There are many different plot devices in mystery stories and scripts which have been recycled over the years. Occasionally, a highly original one is used. In this activity, students are given plot devices and asked to incorporate them into a story or script.

Variations and follow-up activities focus on plot 'cliches' and genres.

Plotting a mystery

Description

Plot a non-violent mystery which depends upon timing and mix-ups.

Mapping

Draw a timetable to show where each character was at all times in the story. Or you may prefer to use a map, with little figures for your characters. Move them to important scenes. You also need a 'twist' for the ending, so that the reader will respond

ASPECT OF CREATIVITY
- Originality
- Lateral thinking
- Logical thinking (deductive reasoning, hypothetical thinking)
- Evaluation (road testing)

KLA FOCUS
- Mathematics
- SOSE
- English

AGE SUITABILITY
- Years 4–12

RESOURCES AND PREPARATION
- Read some mysteries and analyse the plotting. Characters in most mysteries are based on a sleuth, a suspect and a 'doer' of the deed. Something usually goes wrong. The sleuth wants to solve the mystery out of curiosity, to clear their own name or for a reward. Often the suspect's alibi depends upon proving that they were somewhere else at a particular time. The motives of the 'doer' are often similar to those of the sleuth – for recognition, reward, revenge, altruistic reasons or pressures from others.

with, Ah, I didn't think of that at first, but yes, it could be right, considering the clues in the story.'

Viewpoint

It is important to decide on the viewpoint from which the story will be told. If you tell it from the sleuth's point of view, the reader will learn the facts as the sleuth uncovers them. If you tell it from the 'doer's' viewpoint, then the reader will know more than the sleuth.

The mystery can be told in the third person (s/he said) which enables the reader to go into the head of one particular character or into the heads of all the characters and know everything that is happening.

Time clues

Choose one or more of the following time clues to include in your mystery.

- A storm destroys the answering machine or e-mail, yet the caller assumes the message has been left and will be acted upon.
- An electrical storm destroys the phone connection. Callers get engaged signals, so assume the person is there.
- The re-dial button is pressed in order to find out who was called last.
- Someone has pre-dialled a number in order to answer a radio competition quickly.
- A difference in time zones. Or use of Daylight Savings Time.

Suspect mix-up

Choose one or more of the following 'mix-ups' to include in your mystery.

- Look-alikes, e.g. people who are physically similar (twins), people with the same colour hair, etc.
- People wearing a costume, e.g. Easter Bunny, Santa Claus, etc.
- Noticeable accessories, e.g. strangely shaped glasses, an eye patch, a nose-ring, etc.

- Someone in uniform – people tend to look at the uniform and what it represents rather than the person, e.g. parking officer, police officer, ambulance officer, pilot, nurse, etc.

Place mix-ups

Choose one or more of the following 'mix-ups' to include in your mystery.

- Names that sound alike, e.g. a character hears and acts upon, 'Meet you up at the Black Hall' when the speaker really meant, 'Meet you at Upper Black Hall' which is a totally different place. Consequently, they miss each other.
- Directions are not clear, e.g. a character is told, 'The package will be left on the right-hand side of the gate' (the right-hand side depends on which way you are going).
- Transposition (or turning the information around the wrong way), e.g. 'Leave the envelope at the first office on the second floor.' A confused courier might leave it at the second office on the first floor. Another possible complication is that some buildings start numbering their floors at ground level. Hence, the first floor is actually ground level. Others call the first storey the first floor. The envelope could be left on the wrong floor.

VARIATIONS AND FOLLOW-UP

- Students record their mystery, complete with sound effects, on an audio recorder. They could then play this to a trial group to see if they can isolate the clues.
- Students 'road test' their mystery by giving it to two other students to read. If they need to, they can then rewrite it in order to 'fix' the logic and make the mystery more believable.
- Using the same plot, students rewrite the story from the viewpoint of another character.

- Analyse mystery stories, plays, films, etc. and make a list of the most commonly used plot devices. Can they be categorised in some way, e.g. 'the luggage mix-up' device, 'the unexpected arrival' device. Which devices have become 'cliched'? What is a cliche? Why are they perceived unfavourably?

- Plotting a story where the sleuth and the 'doer' are the same person is one of the most technically difficult plots to plan. Students should consider the viewpoint, and when and whether the reader will 'know' the dual roles. For this type of mystery, students could plot in pairs. They could then swap their story with another pair who check certain technical aspects. List the aspects you want pairs to check, e.g. 'When did you realise it was the same person? How did you realise? What was the clue that gave the secret away?

PMI (Pluses, Minuses, Intriguing aspects)

PMI is a creative thinking strategy originally proposed by Edward de Bono. Technically speaking, it is a logical skill, but students need to be able to evaluate what they have produced. They also need the skill of analysing what has been suggested before, so that when they are trying to improve a product or idea, they can tell what aspects have been successful or unsuccessful in the past. To sum up PMI, students evaluate ideas, proposals, products or solutions by looking at the 'Pluses', the 'Minuses' and the 'Intriguing aspects'.

Starters

Students can use a PMI analysis on a created product, solution or idea. They can also use it to evaluate interesting propositions and ideas created by others such as their classmates, or by famous

ASPECT OF CREATIVITY
- Evaluation
- Logical thinking (logical application)

KLA FOCUS
- English
- Science
- Arts
- Mathematics
- Music
- SOSE
- LOTE
- Health and Physical Education

AGE SUITABILITY
- Years K–9

RESOURCES AND PREPARATION
- Model the process.

or expert persons. Students can use any of the following 'starters' to evaluate, using the PMI strategy:

- compulsory measles vaccination for all children
- compulsory flu vaccination for all people
- arranged marriages
- five-year marriage licences which have to be renewed or they lapse
- body piercing
- private ownership of sporting teams
- virtual reality advertisements, e.g. where TV viewers see an ad superimposed on the walls of a football stadium during a match
- re-usable gift-wrapping paper
- no insurance pay-out if a policy holder suicides
- legal age for driving, marriage, drinking alcohol or voting to be lowered
- a law is passed that men and women pay exactly the same price for a haircut
- advertisements on toilet rolls
- only open fires are allowed as heating
- banning paper tissues
- computerised electronic home jailing (a device on the leg)
- compulsory school milk
- phone calls which cut you off after three minutes
- every student is paid five dollars a day to attend school
- criminals have property seized to pay for the police force
- reintroduction of a town crier
- a bath plug that changes colour and displays the word 'hot' once the temperature tops 44°C
- a surcharge of a dollar for anyone who wants to use the new 'no waiting' facility at a supermarket.

VARIATIONS AND FOLLOW-UP

- Students submit ideas and suggestions (in a suggestion box) to be evaluated using the PMI strategy.
- Use the PMI strategy to evaluate students' own products or solutions.
- Use the PMI strategy to evaluate 'backyard' items, e.g. the school fete, an excursion, local community issues, etc.

Postcode artist*

This is another activity which focuses on artistic creativity. And it is lots of fun! Students draw pictures which others decode in order to find the name of Australian towns in the postcode book (available at any local post office). There is also a strong emphasis on problem-solving, and the need to consider the impact of what is drawn on others who are trying to decode it.

What to do

Using a postcode book, students select two Australian towns and draw each town's name, e.g. the town of Hartwell could be drawn as a heart with a tick. Drawings are displayed around the room. Students write their guess on a folded piece of paper accompanied by their name. Each guess is then put in a paper bag or box beneath the appropriate drawing. It is important to remind students to consider the people trying to decipher the postcode, and therefore, they should not make their drawings too obscure.

ASPECT OF CREATIVITY
- Originality
- Logical thinking (logical application)

KLA FOCUS
- Arts
- English
- Mathematics

AGE SUITABILITY
- Years 3–9

RESOURCES AND PREPARATION
- As many postcode books or White Pages phone directories as you can locate. (Alternatively, students can make their selection from their phone book at home.)

VARIATIONS AND FOLLOW-UP

- ◊ Students can do follow-up research on:
  - ~ the rules for postcodes – is there a better system?
  - ~ phone prefixes
  - ~ maps – who makes them and how?
  - ~ street directories.
- ◊ Students can dress up as a country town's name.
- ◊ Students can design a holiday trip or treasure hunt using only postcodes, not names.
- ◊ Using their own body shapes, students can mime the number of a postcode, e.g. 4180

* Postcode artist is based on a similar but more detailed group game for teaching social skills see *Dirty Tricks: Classroom Games for Teaching Social Skills* by Helen McGrath, Addison Wesley Longman, 1996.

POSTER!
Creative problem-solving

This activity follows steps towards a creative solution to a problem, and helps students to understand and remember the creative problem-solving process. There is a POSTER acronym on Template 6 (see p 121) which can be used to help students direct the process. The essence of a 'good problem' (to be used with this technique) is that there must be no one correct answer, nor simple solution.

The POSTER model

POSTER stands for:

Problem

Options

Solution selection

Target plan

Evaluate short-term progress

Review and revamp in the longer term

ASPECT OF CREATIVITY
- Flexibility
- Originality
- Looking at the big picture (consider all factors, consider all the people)

KLA FOCUS
- English
- Science
- Arts
- Mathematics
- Music
- SOSE
- LOTE
- Health and Physical Education

AGE SUITABILITY
- Years 2–12

RESOURCES AND PREPARATION
- Training in the POSTER strategy.

The POSTER model directs students to look at the situation and the facts, and then suggests problem-solving steps based on:

- identifying the main problem
- generating solution options
- selecting one solution to try
- making a target plan to implement the selected solution
- evaluating the progress of the solution along the way
- reviewing how successful the solution was after a specified time period.

Using each of the sub-headings and questions on Template 6 (see p 121), students apply them directly to the problem. They may need to do some research, conduct interviews or even visit the site of the problem. They can work in pairs, small groups or individually, and can report their findings to the class. Findings and ideas can be collated on the whiteboard, a computer or in a place where others may add their comments. The length of time per project may vary considerably from one session to a few days or even weeks.

TEMPLATE 6
THE POSTER STRATEGY

Describe it!

Situations
- Where is this occurring?
- What is the big picture?

Facts
- Who?
- How?
- What?
- How many?
- Where?
- When not?
- When?

Now POSTER it!

Problem
- How many problems are there? Restate each.
- Which are the most and least important problems or parts?

Options
- Brainstorm all possible solutions, no matter how silly they seem.
- Don't evaluate them yet, just accept them. No answers are wrong.
- Think laterally.
- 'Piggyback' on each others' ideas.

Solution selection
- State criteria for a good solution.
- Evaluate each idea by applying the criteria and thinking through the implications. Identify the strengths and weaknesses of each. (A criteria grid could also be used to compare different solutions.)
- Select one to try.

Target plan
- Develop an action plan, predict difficulties and then try your plan.

Evaluate short-term progress
- How is it going? What is working well and what does not seem to be working? What needs fixing?

Review and revamp in the longer term
- Is it working? What needs to be 'fine-tuned'?

Here is an example of how POSTER can be used with the following problem:

Describe it!

Problem: School and public library theft of the most 'in demand' materials.

Despite barcodes and other security measures, students and readers are cutting or removing crucial and much-sought-after pages from texts, and smuggling them out of school and public libraries. This is draining library funds as replacement books have to be bought and security staff need to be paid. These extra funds could have otherwise been used to purchase additional books and services.

Situations

Where is this occurring?

The reference-page theft is occurring in the school library and the public library. Despite Internet use of digital references, some texts are still only used in print formats.

What is the big picture?

Extracts from recommended, expensive medical and legal texts are needed at the same time by large numbers of students. Copies are in short supply and most students can't afford to buy them. 'Honest' students are frustrated and fearful that they will not be able to find or use the resources. This means arguments are common between competing students and the number of complaints to library staff has risen.

Facts

Who?

Complaints mainly from students studying popular subjects with high enrolments or rare resources.

What?

Crucial pages cut from expensive texts.

Where?

In public and school libraries.

When?

During library service hours.

How?

By scissor or knife.

How many?

Multiple copies exist of the most crucial texts. Approximately half have been cut or damaged.

When not? *(Conditions under which books or pages are less likely to be stolen.)*

When students are encouraged to report incidents.

Electronic scanner picks up metallic objects such as scissors or knife. Surveillance cameras installed.

Now POSTER it!

Problem

What is it? Restate it.

Increasing cost to replace and monitor the use of popular library texts.

How many problems are there?

- Approximately half of the copies have been mutilated.
- Genuine students have lost the opportunity to use relevant texts.
- Library costs are increasing.
- Page thieves are getting away with their crimes.
- Money is being wasted on electronic surveillance instead of on the information students need.

Which are the most and least important bits?

- Genuine students have lost the opportunity to use relevant texts.
- Library costs are increasing.

Options

Brainstorm all possible solutions, no matter how silly they seem.

- Provide extra photocopies of the 'in-demand' pages at the desk.
- Readers and students sign for use.
- Encourage teachers to stagger the dates of assignments and required reading, so that all students are not seeking the same books at the same time.
- Students can lease texts for the semester.
- Texts can be downloaded from the Internet or made available digitally.
- Re-organise bookshelves.

Don't evaluate them yet, just accept them. No answers are wrong.

- Install more photocopiers.
- Make the punishment fit the crime for the thieves.
- Close the library.

Think laterally.

- Ban knives or scissors (even for library staff).
- Insist on only see-through bags.
- Make thieves copy out pages by hand multiple times for other students.
- Have a student thief write an anonymous article for the school newspaper about why the pages were stolen. Ask for reply letters.
- Start an e-mail discussion on the Internet asking for solutions which have worked elsewhere.
- Provide a 'recycling' bin for ex-thieves to return used pages, at no penalty.

Solution selection
State criteria for a good solution.
- Cost effective.
- Doesn't alienate or disadvantage honest users.
- Doesn't violate rights.
- Evaluate each idea by applying criteria. Then select one.
- Electronic downloading of crucial pages is selected.

Target plan
Develop an action plan based around the selected solution.
- Electronic downloading of crucial pages — fees paid to authors in lieu of royalties.
- Difficulties could be staff resistance and student lack of skill.

Evaluate short-term progress
How is it going and what still needs fixing?
- Twenty per cent fewer complaints.
- Students complain that they can't get enough access to the Internet to download.
- Titles of texts in demand keep changing.

Review and revamp in the longer term
What are the new facts?
- Forty per cent fewer complaints after three months.

Is it working? What needs to be 'fine-tuned'?
- Yes, but not perfectly.
- Will need greater access to the Internet.
- Asking teachers to give more photocopied material or links in class will help.

Problem starters

Here are some problems which work well with this strategy.

Snail mail

Snails in a local area are eating the mail in letterboxes. How can you keep the mail safe and at the same time not kill or maim the snails? Certain crucial letters have been nibbled beyond legibility.

Park right

The local shopping complex continually receives complaints about the car park. These relate to long waits for a space, fights over limited car spaces, inefficient movement between areas, disabled parks being used by others etc. There is no more land on which to build more car-parking space. How can they improve the parking situation so that it is as fair and as efficient as possible, given that there are usually more shoppers with cars than there are car spaces?

Ticket queue

When grand final or rock concert tickets become available, ticket agencies encourage queuing for a long time ahead of the release of tickets. Imagine that queuing has been banned. Create a fair and efficient system for allocating tickets.

Bed rock

An older sister is always playing her favourite music very loudly, late at night. A younger brother and sister are supposed to go to bed earlier, but are kept awake by the music. The house has three bedrooms – the parents share one and the three children must share the remaining two. Little brother sleeps through anything but little sister is getting cranky due to disturbed sleep. All three argue a lot. The walls are thin and noise travels.

Big sister has always been a 'night owl' and gets up later in the morning than the rest of the family. Earplugs, changing rooms, playing equally loud classical music and noise curfews have all been discussed. How can the problem be solved?

Stock take

The supermarket has been losing stock due to shoplifters. Uncertain whether staff are involved, management wants to try new methods to reduce theft. Certain types of goods are being taken, mainly expensive chocolates, cosmetics and meats. These come from different aisles. Electronic surveillance cameras and undercover security staff have not found reasons for the increased loss. What can be done to expose the culprit or culprits?

Blood flow

Blood supplies are low in all categories. Hospitals and medical centres are worried that if an emergency occurs there will not be enough reserve blood available. There have been unfounded rumours about the dangers of infection when donating blood and this has reduced the number of donors. Until now, there has been a minimum age for donating. How can more donors be encouraged?

Melt down

Heating and cooling costs have soared in the new building where 1,000 people work. Unless running costs are reduced, staff will have to be retrenched. How might you reduce these costs — by changing people's habits, and/or by changing the type of heating or cooling systems? What other ways could be explored?

Paper trail

Huntsville High School has a large stationery bill. Unless paper is re-used within the school there will be no money left for paper purchases in third term. How could staff, students and parents be encouraged to re-use paper?

ID

Most people dislike wearing name tags which fall off or stick to the wrong places. The huge 'Back-to-Old Country Town' festival is to be held. Many people will need to know the names of others at the festival. Some women may have changed their surnames when they were married and will now need to show their previous surname, too. Others will need to show their job roles at the festival. In order for the festival to run smoothly, how could the problem of getting people to design and wear name tags they like be solved?

Supermarket rage

The local supermarket has been experiencing an increased number of enraged customers. They are loudly cross with the fact that staff reductions are causing great delays at the checkout. Customers also get cross at the inefficient way in which a new cashier comes on when the queues get long. And they don't want to use the electronic self serve queues. Staff usually invite the last people in the adjacent queue to come across and they serve them ahead of the people who have been waiting some time. How could 'supermarket rage' be reduced?

Music to buy books by

You have taken over the management of a large shop which sells books, magazines, small gifts and stationery items. You have to choose suitable music to play in the shop. Consider all factors. Consider all the people. What will you choose?

VARIATIONS AND FOLLOW-UP

- ◇ Students propose problems to be used.
- ◇ Select problems which relate to a current topic. For example, if the focus is on the environment the problem could be, 'How can we get people to reduce the amount of paper tissues and paper towels they use?' If the focus is on genetics, the problem might be, 'How

could we make sure that people with the same genetic defect do not reproduce?'

❖ Students can use Template 7 (see p 130) when they are comparing possible solutions. Criteria A to D may vary, but will probably be selected from:
- cost
- humaneness and respect for others
- convenience
- appeal
- looks
- time
- legal correctness.

TEMPLATE 7
SOLUTION CRITERIA

Please note: selection criteria (1–10, with 10 being best)

Possibilities	Criteria A:	Criteria B:	Criteria C:	Criteria D:	Total scores
Solution 1					
Solution 2					
Solution 3					
Solution 4					
Solution 5					

Private eye

These activities are fun! Students are given detailed scenarios and encouraged to deduce, from the clues available, what might have happened.

They need to give good, rational reasons for their deductions. They then create their own scenarios for others to solve.

Scenarios to use

Students, working with a partner, become the 'private eyes' who solve the mystery. A crime scenario is provided, but pairs may add extra details. Drawing on their skills of deduction, they are asked:

- What do you think happened and why? (They should mention the clues they used to come to this conclusion.)
- What caused it?
- What do you think happened after the crime was committed?
- Who do you think is involved?

ASPECT OF CREATIVITY
- Logical thinking (deductive reasoning, hypothetical thinking)
- Flexibility

KLA FOCUS
- English
- Science

AGE SUITABILITY
- Years 4–12

RESOURCES AND PREPARATION
- Discuss the role of an investigator at a crime scene.
- Discuss the differences between evidence (facts) and hearsay (gossip).

Students must be able to give sound rational reasons for each conclusion they draw.

Crime scenario 1

(Clues: spinning wheel, broken glass, red stiletto)

A bike wheel is spinning on a wet country road. The rest of the bike is missing. There are car skid marks across the centre line of the road. A red stiletto shoe sits amidst broken glass on the roadside. In the distance a car engine can be heard.

Crime scenario 2

(Clues: ring, roof, rain, ripped card)

There is a bad storm on a winter afternoon. Rain is pouring down. The gutters are overloaded. Suddenly, water gushes from the old downpipe and a soggy, ripped card swirls out. Then a gold ring is flushed out!

Crime scenario 3

(Clues: number 13, personalised number plate, a four-leaf clover, Friday the 13th)

It was Friday the 13th. Cars were stopped at the traffic lights near the fruit and vegetable market. In front, was a car with LUCKY as a personalised number plate. The green truck going to market and carrying possibly one four-leaf clover amongst its load, didn't stop in time. It crashed into LUCKY and yet there were no brake marks!

Designing crime scenarios

Students can design their own crime scenarios, using the following clues:

- elephant, bath, trumpet, net
- leg with a cut, ice cubes, chain
- torn envelope with sender's address, business card, lipstick mark
- one-way mirror, muddy footprints, mobile phone

- disk, rubbish bin, scream on tape
- e-mail message, torn cheque, pressed flower
- jewellery box, lipstick message on window, shattered clock
- skid on road, broken brick fence, siren
- still bouncing ball, shopping trolley, fire extinguisher
- purple hanky, green glass, white camellia
- wet towel, carrot cake with bite missing, locker token
- damp hair, wrinkled T-shirt, first-aid kit open
- tree trunk with rings showing, sharp axe, 'Contest' notice
- one sneaker, freezer door open, candle burning
- stopped clock, melting ice-cream, answer phone off
- voice message saying 'Help!', background noise of motor, red light
- band aid, stains on hand, briefcase with number lock, map marked with a cross
- room keys to 801 and 108, passport with the wrong photo, unusual opal ring.

VARIATIONS AND FOLLOW-UP

- Students can undertake follow-up research on:
  - forensic science and forensic medicine
  - the role of coroners, and the rules governing autopsies and inquests
  - private investigators and their licensing rules and restrictions
  - the genre of detective novels
  - famous fictional detectives – what do they all have in common/how are they different? (students can make a comparison grid)
  - why people are so fond of detective stories (students can conduct interviews or carry out a survey and collate their data)
  - famous criminal cases which have involved intensive forensic detection
  - famous unsolved crimes.

Recipe parodies

Parodies require humorous creativity. Students have always loved them, and they feature strongly in the schoolyard, as June Factor's books *All Right*, *Vegemite* and *Far Out Brussel Sprout* attest! Most of us have giggled at the creative cleverness of parodies such as 'On Top of Spaghetti' or 'Jingle Bells, Batman Smells', etc. In this activity, students are asked to use creative parody in a simple form by putting together simple parodies using a recipe structure.

What is a parody?

A parody is a satire which follows a known shape or structure, but updates or changes the content. A common source of parody is 'The Twelve Days of Christmas' where the original words are changed for others, e.g. Australian animals or ones which represent a play on words (e.g. '… and a bar fridge in the pantry'). People enjoy a parody more when they know the original upon which it was based. The aim of a parody can be varied — to amuse, 'send up', entertain

ASPECT OF CREATIVITY
- Elaboration
- Flexibility
- Logical thinking (analogical thinking) originality

KLA FOCUS
- English

AGE SUITABILITY
- Years 3–9

RESOURCES AND PREPARATION
- Use an example to explain that parody is a 'send up' or a humorous adaptation of a previously created poem, song or structure. Use one of poet Ogden Nash's parodies as an example.

or criticise. Many playground songs and rhymes are examples of parodies.

Recipes as parodies

A recipe offers a well-known pattern for grouping ingredients but it can be used for grouping ideas. The original recipe might be for making pancakes. However, students can use its structure to write a recipe for something else. Students can create a 'Recipe for a friend' following the headings of a 'real' recipe. So, instead of writing about how to make pancakes, for example, the recipe will list the ingredients for a friend.

Name of recipe:

Recipe for a good friendship

Ingredients:

2 cups of loyalty

3 spoonfuls of honesty

1 litre of listening

Method:

Mix in with lots of fun.

Spend lots of time making sure the mix is right.

After having a go at writing 'Recipe for a good friendship', students could tackle one of the following titles:

- formula for getting into the team
- formula for getting a role in the play
- recipe for writing a best-seller
- recipe for a hero
- pollution cocktail
- recipe for a healthy lifestyle
- recipe for being a 'hit' with the opposite sex.

VARIATIONS AND FOLLOW-UP

✧ Other useful structures which students can adapt, 'send up' or criticise, include:
  - nursery rhymes
  - well-known songs or anthems, e.g. Advance Australia Fair', 'Waltzing Matilda', 'Jingle Bells', 'Three Blind Mice'
  - playground rhymes
  - football songs.

Renovator's delight

In this activity, students design ways in which buildings, rooms, furniture and machinery may be modified for a specific stated purpose.

This requires some degree of artistic creativity as well as creative problem-solving and flexible thinking.

Renovating ideas

Students can modify an item or idea for a specific purpose and then draw it. The following list of ideas can be used by students:

- safety-proof your bedroom for a just walking toddler
- equip a kitchen for a blind person
- modify a school desk to make it more appealing to students
- modify a car to make it better for children on long trips
- turn your garage into a bedroom

ASPECT OF CREATIVITY
- Flexibility
- Elaboration
- Originality

KLA FOCUS
- SOSE
- Technology Arts

AGE SUITABILITY
- Years K–12

RESOURCES AND PREPARATION
- Introduce the topic of renovation and modification.

- turn a part of your school into a restaurant
- use your wardrobe to incorporate a sound system
- design a bathroom which can convert to a spare bedroom
- turn a shoe box into a toy
- convert a bike for delivering newspapers or for taking your pet on trips with you
- redesign a blind, curtain or doona so that it has at least three different uses
- design a cubby house from what's in your classroom.

VARIATIONS AND FOLLOW-UP

- Students can research:
    - the rules governing house renovations
    - what happens if someone next-door renovates or builds in a way which blocks out your light or your view
    - what makes people renovate (interviews or surveys could be useful here)
    - how old buildings are renovated and what rules govern such renovations.
- Students could also:
    - describe and/or draw how they would renovate their own bedroom if they were given $10,000 for the renovations (they can't spend the money on computer equipment!)
    - produce a 'before and after' photographic display of the renovations
    - photograph a particular room or building and describe and/or draw how they would like to renovate it.

SAMs (Similes, Analogies, and Metaphors)

Developing an analogy requires logical thinking, as the task is to identify how two things are similar enough in enough ways, to be considered analogous (e.g. writing a book is analogous to being pregnant). However, there is also a great deal of creative thinking required, as there are so many choices when making analogous links.

In order to create an original link, one must have some understanding of what links people have made before. So many 'cliches' are actually over-used analogies, e.g. 'He drew the short straw.' This activity gives students practice in making analogous links. This process also develops the use of similes and metaphors in writing.

How to develop SAMs

Students work with a partner to develop similes, analogies and/or metaphors in response to specific concepts. They should

ASPECT OF CREATIVITY
- Originality
- Evaluation (criteria grid)
- Flexibility
- Logical thinking (logical application)

KLA FOCUS
- English

AGE SUITABILITY
- Years 4–12

RESOURCES AND PREPARATION
- Discuss the concepts of analogies, similes and metaphors.
- Discuss cliches.
- Collect and share good examples of cliches, similes and metaphors.

at first list the attributes of the chosen concept, and then think analogically and creatively to come up with unusual, but accurate ways in which other concepts are similar.

Students list all the possible attributes of a dentist. For example:

- wears a white coat
- works with fillings
- does root canal work
- can cause pain
- often charges a lot of money
- uses anaesthetic
- can replace mouth parts with false ones
- endures bad breath
- looks up people's noses
- says 'open wide' a lot
- scrapes off debris
- drills.

Then, next to each attribute, students write down what other kinds of people or things also have that attribute in a major way. They then use the list to complete, in as many ways as possible, the following sentence:

A dentist is like a _____ because they both _____

A dentist is like an *archaeologist* because they both *dig at the roots*.

A dentist is like a *gold miner* because they both *do extractions*.

A dentist is like a *land filler* because they both *fill in holes*.

A dentist is like an *oil rigger* because they both *drill*.

A dentist is like a *person who surprises you* because they both *cause your jaw to drop*.

Each pair develops a number of responses. They then select their two best responses and use a criteria grid (see Template 8 see p 142) to select the one that works the best. Students should be encouraged to make sure that their comparison is accurate, unusual and appealing.

SAM ideas

- A doctor is like a _____ because they both _____
- A circus is like a _____ because they both _____
- A family is like a _____ because they both _____
- A school is like a _____ because they both _____
- A zoo is like a _____ because they both _____
- A teacher is like a _____ because they both _____
- A kaleidoscope is like a _____ because they both _____
- An airport is like a _____ because they both _____
- A garden is like a _____ because they both _____

VARIATIONS AND FOLLOW-UP

- Students can submit ideas for comparison based on a current classroom topic, e.g. if the focus is on Antarctica, students might suggest:

  An iceberg is like _____ because _____

- Students put together a display using photographs or drawings of two analogous items with the links written underneath.

TEMPLATE 8
EVALUATING SAM

Please note: selection criteria (1–10, with 10 being best)

Criteria	SAM A	SAM B
Accuracy (1-10)		
Appeal (1-10)		
Originality (1-10)		
Total score		

Criteria	SAM A	SAM B
Accuracy (1-10)		
Appeal (1-10)		
Originality (1-10)		
Total score		

SCRUMPTIOUS

This activity offers the acronym SCRUMPTIOUS to help students think creatively about how they might improve or elaborate on a specified product. This kind of skill is used by inventors and creative directors in marketing departments. In the commercial world, there is often 'nothing new under the sun', but the amendments and variations allow for a 'newness' or novelty which appeals to customers. A 'Variations and follow-up' activity focuses on technological improvements over time in our culture.

How to apply SCRUMPTIOUS

Laminate the SCRUMPTIOUS acronym on Template 9 (see p 146). Make sure all students have access to this information. In groups of three, students decide how they can improve upon a product. They should try to find as many ways as possible. Students should follow the three procedures below.

ASPECT OF CREATIVITY
- Elaboration
- Logical thinking (logical application)

KLA FOCUS
- Mathematics
- Arts
- Technology

AGE SUITABILITY
- Years 3–9

RESOURCES AND PREPARATION
- Model the process using a classroom chair as an example.

- Groups list all the things that could be changed by referring to SCRUMPTIOUS on Template 9 (see p 146).
- After all the suggested changes, students select the versions that they like, then finalise and draw their new and improved product.
- Students are then allocated to another group to work with. Using the criteria grid on Template 10 (see p 147), they write their product in the first column (Product A) and the product of the other group in the second column (Product B). They then make an evaluative comparison by discussing each product's similarities and differences. Scores are then given to each product. Alternatively, all groups can rate each other's products.

Starting ideas

- picnic basket
- school sunhat
- sunglasses case
- garbage bin
- fountain
- diary
- phone
- kettle
- backpack
- desk
- school locker
- dog kennel or cat basket
- hanging basket
- bed
- pencil case
- escalator
- coat for travelling
- clothes line

VARIATIONS AND FOLLOW-UP

◊ Students can suggest theme-related objects to use with SCRUMPTIOUS, e.g. if a unit of study is on electricity, a desk lamp could be used.

◊ Students can take a common household product and draw an approximate timeline to show the improvements made over time. They will need to interview parents and grandparents. Here are some possible ideas:
  - toasters
  - washing machines
  - sound systems
  - irons
  - hair dryers
  - answering machines.

◊ Use the following task with students.

◊ There is a message on your answering machine from 'New Inventions Incorporated' asking if there is anyone in your household who has thought of a new or improved product. You therefore decide to create an improved version of a household item or appliance in order to finance an up-and-coming holiday. Look around, choose an item and use SCRUMPTIOUS (see Template 9, p 146) to improve it.

◊ Do a PMI (see p 114) on the strategy used above for soliciting new or improved products and ideas.

TEMPLATE 9
SCRUMPTIOUS

S   Size and shape

C   Colour and contrasts

R   Rearrange the parts

U   Uses other than this one

M   Mass and material

P   Presentation of product to others

T   Texture, trims and turns

I   Inserts, fasteners, pockets and locks

O   Operation of the parts – can it be altered?

U   User-friendly aspects

S   Smell

TEMPLATE 10
SCRUMPTIOUS CRITERIA

Please note: selection criteria (1–10, with 10 being best)

Criteria	Product A Creators: 1. 2. 3.	Product B Creators: 1. 2. 3.
Appeal (1–10)		
User-friendliness (1–10)		
Competitiveness How well will it sell compared to other similar products? (1–10)		
Total score		

Sentencing

This activity has a strong logical component as well as a creative one. It aims to get students to apply the logical rules of grammar in a creative way. Students are asked to write grammatically correct and sensible sentences from a series of 'starting' letters. They must form proper sentences and words must be used correctly. Points are allocated according to specific criteria for each sentence. Bonus points are given for unique choices of words to complete the sentence.

How to begin

Students are provided with a word containing four to seven letters, e.g. TRIPS. They are asked to make a sensible and grammatically correct sentence using the letters of the word as the initial letters of each word in the sentence (used in the correct order). Choose words that have at least one vowel (preferably two) for a five-letter word. Make sure that there are three vowels for a six- or seven letter word.

ASPECT OF CREATIVITY
- Fluency (Systematic Alphabetic Generation)
- Originality
- Evaluation (criteria grid)

KLA FOCUS
- English

AGE SUITABILITY
- Years 3–9

RESOURCES AND PREPARATION
- Dictionaries should be made available.
- Decide on suitable words to use. Revise the concept of a sentence.

Start with five-letter words. Bonus points are given for words in the sentence that are unique, in that no-one else in the group has used that word.

What to do

- Choose a word at random and ask students to write a sentence with any theme they choose, e.g. the word GREEN.

   Grasshoppers Roam Each Estate Nocturnally.

   Gigantic Roaches Energetically Enter Norway.

- Alternatively, the word can be related to a current classroom theme, e.g. GREEN ties in with the topic 'Environment'. Or for a 'Travel' theme, the word TRIPS might be chosen; make sure the sense of the sentence relates to journeys, travel, transport or holidays.

   The Road Is Perilous Sometimes.

   This is a challenging way of constructing a sentence.

- A criteria grid can be used to evaluate each sentence (see Template 11 p 151). Students can complete two sentences and use the grid to decide which one is better. Alternatively, they can swap with a partner and rate each other's. Points can be allotted according to the following criteria:
    - unusual choice of word (one point for each word not used by anyone else in the class — sentences will need to be displayed)
    - the appeal of the sentence
    - the logic of the sentence
    - the grammatical correctness of the sentence.

Remind students to use the SAG strategy (Systematic Alphabetic Generation — see p 4) to brainstorm possible words, e.g. when they are trying to find a word which starts with a consonant such as 'T' they can first try writing down words that start with 'Ta' then 'Te' then 'Ti', 'To' and 'Tu'. When looking for a word that starts with a vowel, e.g. 'o' they can systematically combine it with each consonant and then each vowel – 'Ob', 'Oc', 'Od', and so on. Dictionaries and thesauruses can be used.

Starter words

Here are some random words to start with:

- image
- brain
- great
- table
- drive
- animal
- sphere
- answer
- gourmet.

VARIATIONS AND FOLLOW-UP

- In groups of four, students can produce one especially good sentence by pooling their original ideas. All sentences could be written on a sheet of paper and passed to each group to be rated using Template 11 (see p 151).
- Students can individually select their own theme-related words to generate creative sentences which are then displayed.

TEMPLATE 11
SENTENCING CRITERIA

Please note: selection criteria (1–10, with 10 being best)

Criteria	Sentence 1	Sentence 2
Unusual words used (1 point for any word not used by another)		
Appeal (1–10)		
Logic of the sentence (1–10)		
Is the sentence grammatically correct? (2 if it is correct, 1 if it is almost correct, 0 if it is wrong)		
Total score		

Shapemakers*

Kids like to doodle, so do adults when they are on the phone. Shapemakers is a slightly more sophisticated and challenging activity based around doodling. The main focus is on artistic creativity and problem-solving as the activity progresses. Students are given simple, basic shapes which they are required to turn into a whole range of pictorial ideas. They then select their most unusual or thought-provoking drawing and label it. Having to think of a label or title is another way of synthesising or bringing together the major idea threads. It's likely that once a label is chosen, the student may want to stress the aspects of the drawing which fit the title.

ASPECT OF CREATIVITY
- Fluency
- Synectics
- Flexibility
- Evaluation (criteria grid)

KLA FOCUS
- Arts
- English

AGE SUITABILITY
- Years 3–9

RESOURCES AND PREPARATION
- Demonstrate the process by turning a circle into a watch.

What to do

Students draw four circles of the same size and turn each of them into interesting objects or designs. They then select their best drawing and give it a title of no more than four words. The aim is to make the drawing as original as possible, so that no other person creates the same or a similar drawing. Artwork is displayed and evaluated using the criteria grid on Template 12 (see p 154) which compares two pictures at a time. The grid asks for assessments of appeal as well as originality. You will need to discuss beforehand what would make this combination of drawing plus title 'original'.

VARIATIONS AND FOLLOW-UP

- Students use triangles, squares or diamonds.
- Students can make a 'picture story' linking several drawings and using their titles to direct plot and sequence. The titles must appear in the story in some form, even if it is a modified form.

* Shapemakers is based on a similar but more detailed group game for teaching social skills see *Dirty Tricks: Classroom Games for Teaching Social Skills* by Helen McGrath, Addison Wesley Longman, 1996.

TEMPLATE 12
SHAPEMAKERS CRITERIA

Please note: selection criteria (1–10, with 10 being best)

Criteria	Drawing 1 Title:	Drawing 2 Title:
Appeal of the drawing (1–10)		
Appeal of the title (1–10)		
How original do you think the drawing and title together are? (1–10)		
Total score		

Criteria	Drawing 1 Title:	Drawing 2 Title:
Appeal of the drawing (1–10)		
Appeal of the title (1–10)		
How original do you think the drawing and title together are? (1–10)		
Total score		

Six Thinking Hats

This activity is based on the well-known strategy by Edward de Bono — a strategy which has been used extensively in the corporate and industrial world. Each of the six hats represents a different way of thinking about a problem. The White Hat represents thinking about the facts. The Black Hat and the Yellow Hat are about negative and positive evaluation. The Red Hat is about feelings. Although some of the hats reflect logical thinking, which is one important element of the creative process, one of the thinking approaches is directly related to creativity — namely the Green Hat, which is about new ideas and modifications. The Blue Hat is thinking about thinking.

Provide students with problems to solve. Have them use the Six Thinking Hats strategy on Template 13 (see p 156) to find some creative solutions to the problem. Use the White, Black, Red and Yellow Hats first. Then use the Blue and Green Hats.

ASPECT OF CREATIVITY
- Flexibility
- Logical thinking (logical application)
- Looking at the big picture (consider all factors, consider all the people)

KLA FOCUS
- English
- Science
- Arts
- Mathematics
- Music
- SOSE
- LOTE
- Health and Physical Education

AGE SUITABILITY
- Years 1–12

RESOURCES AND PREPARATION
- Demonstrate the process with the idea of free lollies given to kids each day at school.

TEMPLATE 13

SIX THINKING HATS

White Hat (think of a blank white sheet of paper)

The White Hat focuses on facts and information.

- What information do we have?
- What information is missing?
- How do we get the information we need?

This is a factual hat so objectivity is the focus.

Red Hat (think of a passionate red heart)

The Red Hat is for our emotions, feelings, hunches and intuitions of the moment. It is possible to report mixed feelings. For example:

- I like this because … but
- I have a hunch that …
- My first response to the idea is …
- I think people will feel …

Black Hat (think of a black cloud)

The Black Hat is the critical hat. It is concerned with the negatives

- Does it fit? (with our values, goals, etc.)
- Will it work?
- What are the dangers and problems?
- What could go wrong?

This is a logical hat so reasons must be given.

Yellow Hat (think of sunshine)

The Yellow Hat focuses on positives.

- What are the benefits?
- Why should it work?
- Can this be done?
- What are the positive outcomes?

This is a logical hat so reasons must be given.

Green Hat (think of greener grass)

The Green Hat focuses on creative improvement.

- What could we change?
- What could we add?
- What if we …?
- What else could we do?

The other hats can then be used to assess the new ideas.

Blue Hat (think of a police officer's uniform)

The Blue Hat is the conductor of the 'thinking orchestra' and focuses on the thinking that is being done.

- Where are we now?
- How far have we got?
- What is the next step?
- Can we have a summary?
- How are we going?
- Which hats do we need to use more?

Ideas to use

Here are some propositions and ideas to use:

- bar-coded road toll collection
- compulsory training for all women in self-defence
- cosmetic surgery
- a breathalyser on your car which disables your car if you fail the test
- genetic assessment of self and relatives for medical insurance to determine any 'predispositions' even in the absence of current illness
- uniforms for teachers
- abolition of the wearing of valuable jewellery to reduce muggings and robberies
- flexitime, i.e. choose when you work your weekly hours
- rostered days off
- a compulsory test to detect suicide risk in children
- crèches
- viral warfare
- compulsory aerobics in schools for half an hour per day
- since SAD (Seasonal Affective Disorder) occurs because of lack of exposure to natural light in winter, a rule has been passed to ban curtains and blinds so that more light can get to people
- a limit of two children per family
- virtual reality advertising (where a laser image is superimposed, for example, on the wall of a sports stadium while a game is being played)
- personal ownership of a sports team
- a children's radio station or a radio station at your school
- conscription.

VARIATIONS AND FOLLOW-UP

- Students use theme-related propositions or ideas.
- In groups of three, each student speaks from the perspective of two hats. Then they swap and speak from the perspective of a different two hats. Remember to use the White, Yellow and Green Hats first.
- Use props such as hats with coloured ribbons, coloured tokens, coloured stickers or badges
- Ask students to create a new hat to think through. What colour would it be? What kind of thinking does it represent?
- Students can design a hat stand which reflects the concept in some way.
- Students can create new versions of the 'Hats' which could be used in schools, e.g. 'six cardboard visors' or 'six stickers on the cheek'.

Top five reasons

Students are asked 'Why?' in regard to questions which have no obvious, simple, factual answer, e.g. 'Why wear earrings?' In order to answer the questions, they have to combine logic and creativity. They then have to decide on their five best answers and rank them. Encourage students to discriminate between more and less effective responses.

Why is a dog house called a kennel?

- The inventor had a dog called Ken
- The word 'ken' means 'know' in Scottish and so we know where the dog is at any given time
- The word originally was 'kernel' meaning 'something which encloses precious things'
- The first company that made a commercial dog house was the Kennel Company
- The first dog houses were below ground more like tunnels. Then someone suggested the dog should be kept above

ASPECT OF CREATIVITY
- Originality
- Logical thinking (deductive reasoning)
- Flexibility

KLA FOCUS
- English
- Science
- Arts
- Mathematics
- Music
- SOSE
- Health and Physical Education

AGE SUITABILITY
- Years 3–9

RESOURCES AND PREPARATION
- No special resources or preparation required.

ground because of mould spores and so it became a 'keep tunnel' and then a 'kennel'.

'Why?' and 'But why?'

Encourage students to use the 'Why?' and 'But why?' approach with this task.

In groups of three, students list all the sound reasons for the following, and then rank them in order of their effectiveness and appeal. They then select the top five reasons.

- Why is a cat referred to as a 'moggy'?
- Why is the cross of the Red Cross red?
- Why do actors say 'good luck' to each other with the expression 'break a leg'?
- Why is 13 an unlucky number?
- Why do we say things come in threes?
- Why are large things referred to as 'jumbo'?
- Why don't men wear skirts or skirt-type clothing in most societies?
- Why is hair colouring traditionally only red, blonde, brown, black or white?
- Why don't we have two-storey cars?
- Why do we finish a meeting by saying 'goodbye'?
- Why do we often say 'bless you' when someone sneezes?
- Why is the noise of a telephone usually called a 'ring'?
- Why are people so fascinated with ESP (Extrasensory perception)?
- Why isn't music compulsory in schools?
- Why is black clothing considered sophisticated?
- Why do people become explorers?
- Where did the saying 'mad as a cut snake' originate?

VARIATIONS AND FOLLOW-UP

✧ Have students give reasons for their top five selection.

✧ Students can rate each other's top five reasons using the criteria grid on Template 14 (see p 162). Discuss the notion of originality in this kind of task beforehand.

TEMPLATE 14

TOP FIVE REASONS CRITERIA

Please note: selection criteria (1–10, with 10 being best)

Reasons:

1 _____
2 _____
3 _____
4 _____
5 _____

Criteria	Reason 1	Reason 2	Reason 3	Reason 4	Reason 5
Overall Appeal (1–10)					
Humour (1–10)					
Logic (1–10)					
Originality (1–10)					
Total score					

Tracking

This activity can be taken outside, or at least parts of it can! Students develop, plan, design, make, play, and/or evaluate games and venues involving the word 'tracking' in all of its meanings. Problem solving 'on site' requires good skills of observation and use of all the senses, as well as creativity.

Two players leave a trail of arrows for another pair to follow. Arrows are left on the ground every 50 metres or so, and can be drawn in the dirt, made of leaves, stones or sticks. 'Markers' could also be left at eye level, e.g. pieces of the same-coloured paper tied to a branch, which are then collected by the people tracking. The first pair of students leave five minutes ahead of the 'trackers'. The aim is to catch up with the first pair before they reach an end point. This can be played in any area where it is not easy to see the first pair leaving their markers or arrows. This usually means a bushland area.

ASPECT OF CREATIVITY
- Originality
- Logical thinking (logical application)
- Flexibility

KLA FOCUS
- Mathematics
- Health and Physical Education
- Science

AGE SUITABILITY
- Years 3–9

RESOURCES AND PREPARATION
- Carry out experiments with types of footprints in moist mud or sand, e.g. running, walking, animals, type of shoe, age of print, weight of person leaving print, direction, bare feet.

What to do

Students design and/or play a game which involves tracking someone or finding a way to somewhere. Consider using beaches, bushlands, parks, etc. Obviously, safety is an issue.

Other possibilities

- Students participate in a treasure hunt where riddle clues are left.
- Students participate in a game based on one student being blindfolded in a limited area. They then use their sense of smell and textual clues to find their way (be cautious here).
- An activity where students visit an area (beach, park, bushland) and draw conclusions from 'clues', e.g. checking out footprints, debris, crushed bushes, crab marks, dead fish, broken twigs, animal droppings, etc. Use the same area with five different groups and compare their conclusions. Remind students not to contaminate the 'evidence'.
- Students participate in a game based on simplified orienteering or rogaining.
- Students participate in a game based on a street directory.

VARIATIONS AND FOLLOW-UP

- Students play 'Facing the Feral!' Inform them that they have been tracked and bailed up by the 'Feral'. They can only reach and use two of the following items to survive:
    ~ a feather
    ~ a white handkerchief
    ~ a pot of pepper
    ~ a jellybean
    ~ a wooden spoon
    ~ a bottle of aftershave
    ~ a gumnut
    ~ a pen.

    They cannot use violence. Students must justify their selection.

- Students can research:
    - tracking
    - getting lost in the desert
    - detective work
    - forensic medicine
    - taking plaster casts of a footprint
    - fossils
    - DNA testing
    - archaeology, e.g. Pompeii
    - voiceprints.
- Students make handprints/footprints in a path, e.g. in concrete, paving blocks, ceramic tiles, etc.
- Students make fingerprints with an ink pad. Compare whorls.

What if ...?

'What if ...?' is often the question which gets many inventors and creative problem-solvers started. Students can tackle this question by combining fanciful possibilities with logical thinking. Students are asked to predict the implications and consequences of slightly absurd hypothetical situations in order to stimulate both processes. The willingness to risk being seen as absurd is often necessary to find a new idea or possibility.

Absurd propositions

Students make predictions based on slightly absurd propositions.

What if...

- we only had one meal per week?
- all girls born in the future were destined to be at least two metres tall?
- all people with the same name had to work together?
- insect populations grew to uncontrollable levels?

ASPECT OF CREATIVITY
- Flexibility
- Imagination
- Logical thinking (hypothetical thinking, deductive reasoning)

KLA FOCUS
- English
- Science
- Arts
- Mathematics
- Music
- SOSE
- Health and Physical Education

AGE SUITABILITY
- Years 4–12

RESOURCES AND PREPARATION
- No resources or preparation are necessary.

- our clothes were edible?
- we could choose our parents?
- the prime minister was chosen on acting ability?
- you had time coupons to spend instead of money?
- the colour green was removed from our environment?
- those with freckles/pimples had the highest status in the country?
- parents and adolescents had to change roles for two months in each year?
- tap water cost more than any other drink?
- music (or reading) was banned?
- refrigeration gases were banned?
- TV/streaming was banned?
- the water supply in your city was contaminated for two weeks?
- people had numbers instead of names?
- everyone was the same height and weight?
- people could only use the wifi when they had generated enough electricity by cycling on a cycle attached to the wifi?
- the city's water supply was polluted for a year?

VARIATIONS AND FOLLOW-UP

- Students propose theme-related 'What if …?' questions, e.g. in a unit on electricity, the question might be, 'What if all homes and businesses could only receive electricity every second day?'

What's one of these?

Students are given items they have never encountered before, and asked to creatively but rationally describe what they are and what they might be used for. Again, students need to take the risk of being seen by their classmates as 'foolish'.

Ideas to use

In groups of three, students generate ideas as to what these undefined objects might be.

They then select their one best answer for each.

What is ...

- a quandong?
- a thinking wall?
- a transit lane in a shop?
- gravelling?
- an aquaresponder?
- cartespure designs?
- a virtual graveyard?
- a grand feather?

ASPECT OF CREATIVITY
- Lateral thinking
- Imagination
- Flexibility
- Logical thinking (deductive reasoning)

KLA FOCUS
- English
- Science
- Arts
- Mathematics
- Music
- SOSE
- Health and Physical Education

AGE SUITABILITY
- Years 4–12

RESOURCES AND PREPARATION
- Model the process using a 'grumpet'.

VARIATIONS AND FOLLOW-UP

- Students propose other abstract things to be described.
- Students bring items which are not well known and others decide what they could be.

Windows of opportunity

'Windows of opportunity' is a lateral thinking strategy in which students are asked to look around them, observe every detail and then use word associations (from the things they see) to solve a problem. This strategy was used frequently while creating appropriate examples for some of the activities in this book and when selecting the title. Even the naming of the strategy was related to the process of looking around and seeing 'windows of opportunity' for openings, instead of 'walls' or 'barriers'.

It is a similar strategy in some ways to Abracadabra words' (see p 23).

Select a problem or task such as the ones listed or those listed in 'POSTER' (see p 119) or 'How many can you think of?' (see p 78) or 'How many ways?' (see p 81) and solve it using word associations.

Use the task of finding a good theme song from songs already composed and recording it for an advertising campaign on protecting the environment.

ASPECT OF CREATIVITY
- Fluency
- Lateral thinking

KLA FOCUS
- English
- Science
- Arts
- Mathematics
- Music SOSE
- Health and Physical Education

AGE SUITABILITY
- Years 3–9

RESOURCES AND PREPARATION
- Model the process for the students.

What to do

- Generate all the solutions you can think of or all the items which fit the criteria.
- When you have exhausted your lists, look slowly around your location at every single detail and use what you see and what it makes you think about to come up with solutions to the task or more items for the list.

Problems and tasks to choose from

- How many songs can you think of which have the word 'me' in the title?
- What could be done to prevent people stealing cutlery from a cafeteria which believes in using stainless steel cutlery rather than plastic?
- How could we encourage students to clean their school shoes each day?
- How could we get more people to job-share?
- How can you improve the school fete?
- How could you improve the school assembly?
- How could we get rid of blowflies?
- How could we get more students to eat breakfast?
- How could we market spinach more successfully?
- How could we stop the ears of an albino cat from being burnt (it licks off sunscreen)?
- How could we sell more thimbles?

VARIATIONS AND FOLLOW-UP

- Students propose appropriate problems and the class compiles a 'Problem Bank'.

- Windows come in all shapes and sizes, as well as different types and thicknesses of glass. Whether double-glazed, stained glass, frosted, open or shut, the image can be a starting point. Demonstrate, in cartoon form, how the strategy of 'Windows of opportunity' works.

Conclusion
Developing a classroom climate which encourages creative thinking

The kind of classroom which encourages students to think creatively has the following characteristics:

- Respect for unusual questions and unusual ideas and products.
- Students who are encouraged to practise and experiment sometimes with evaluation, and sometimes without.
- The teacher structures for and values activities and projects initiated by students.
- There is a 'no-put-down' rule to discourage intolerance of different views.
- Many open-ended tasks, for which there is no correct answer or outcome, are provided.
- Several times each week, some specific time is devoted to tasks which encourage creative thinking.
- Acceptance of the need to take risks and make mistakes is seen as part of the process of learning and improvement.
- The teacher models the idea of following curiosity and taking the risks of being creative and different.

- There is a strong emphasis on having fun with creative thinking and being playful.
- There is a stronger emphasis on cooperation than on competition.
- Opportunities for students to make selections as to what they will do within a particular kind of creative activity.
- There are opportunities to 'debrief' the creative process, e.g. after an activity and in a whole-class format, initiate discussion questions such as, 'Why did you think of that? Was that your first idea or one further down the track? What ideas did the two of you put together to get that solution? What made you curious about that aspect?'
- The teacher identifies the creative principle in each solution, e.g. 'It seems that the first idea is not necessarily the best. Often it is the one that comes later, after you have played around a little. Your idea "piggybacked" on Tom's idea. So two heads were better than one here. So curiosity directed you.'

About the author

Author, mentor and teacher **Hazel Edwards OAM** has been involved with gifted education as an original Tournament of Minds problem-writer and judge. She has mentored interesting thinkers of all ages and is intrigued by the techniques of unconventional problem-solvers. Many of her published stories deal with 'coping successfully with being different' and with real problem solvers such as Antarctic expeditioners. Educators use her books, play scripts and literacy materials but Hazel is best known for 'There's a Hippopotamus on our Roof Eating Cake' classic series. Hazel was awarded the Monash University Distinguished Alumni Award for Education in 2022.

Recent Amba Press publications include:

- *Grief and Loss in Schools: A Resource for Teachers*
- *Issues: A Resource of Play Scripts and Activities for Teachers*
- *Workplays: Work and Career Play Scripts and Activities for Secondary Students*
- *Writing for Young People: The Business of Creativity*
- *Authorpreneurship: The Business of Creativity*

www.ingramcontent.com/pod-product-compliance
Lightning Source LLC
Chambersburg PA
CBHW050416120526
44590CB00015B/1988